grandparenting
the *blended* family

grandparenting
the *blended* family

HOW TO SUCCEED WITH YOUR STEP
OR ADOPTED GRANDCHILDREN

familius

DENE LOW, PHD

Copyright © 2013 by Dene Low

All rights reserved.

Published by Familius LLC, www.familius.com

Familius books are available at special discounts for bulk purchases for sales promotions, family or corporate use. Special editions, including personalized covers, excerpts of existing books, or books with corporate logos, can be created in large quantities for special needs. For more information, contact Premium Sales at 559-876-2170 or email specialmarkets@familius.com

Library of Congress Catalog-in-Publication Data
2013943963

pISBN 978-1-938301-32-2
eISBN 978-1-938301-31-5

Printed in the United States of America

Edited by Brooke Jorden
Cover design by David Miles
Book design by Christopher Taney

10 9 8 7 6 5 4 3 2 1

First Edition

Contents

Introduction i

Grandparents Can Save the World 1

Meet the New Family 21

What Do They Call You? 35

A Step-Grandparent Is Always
(and Even More of) a Parent 43

An Island of Peace 59

Interacting with All the Exes Who
May or May Not Live in Texas 75

Holidays, Traditions, Events—
Oh, My! 89

Politics, Religion, and Other
Times to Shut Up 109

Enriching Lives: When It's Time
to Put Up and Speak Up 123

Going the Distance—
When Families Are Far Apart 137

When Your World Crumbles 149

Conclusion 157

Interviewee Biographies 159

Introduction

I love being a grandparent and all the various roles that come with that title. My role shifts constantly as grandchildren are born, grow up, or come into the family through marriage, re-marriage, or adoption—both formal and informal. Talking with other grandparents gives me ideas for what to do to be a successful grandparent. Their experiences help me, which is how the idea for this book was born. I want to share with you the stories of everyday grandparents who do remarkable things to help their grandchildren. This book is meant to be a resource for inspiration and encouragement for all of us as grandparents.

What does it mean to be a grandparent, especially today, with all the many variations of relationships that come about because of blended families? There are normal grandparents, step-grandparents, adoptive grandparents, and adopted grandparents, and as many combinations of grandparenting as there are people and types of families.

In many cultures, stories of grandparents conjure up images of wise and loving elderly people worth revering, caring for, and going to for comfort and advice. Didn't Little Red Riding Hood take her grandmother goodies, and didn't she risk her life to save her grandmother? Stories about grandparents abound in our own culture, but the stories grandparents like the best are about experiences with grandchildren. We tell them all the time as we share our delight in our grandchildren with others. For example, my friend Melissa told me that she took her three-year-old grandson outside one cold spring morning to work in the garden. He was reluctant to wear his hoodie because the sun was shining so brightly, but after they were outside for a few minutes he was shivering. He complained, "Grandma, Mr. Sun isn't doing his job." Cute, right? And then there are the people who whisk out photographs of grandchildren as soon as the word "grandparent" is mentioned. Maybe you are one of those people. Good for you. That means that you adore your grandchildren, and they will know it.

After interviewing more than thirty people for this book, I am left in awe of the extraordinary lengths so many people go to, in both traditional and blended family situations, to reach out and just plain love the children who come into their lives under so many varied circumstances. The truth is that most of the time we don't have any control over how grandchildren come to us, and we may find ourselves filling roles that we never planned on filling. For example, our son remarried after a divorce and not only gave us the gift of a precious new daughter-in-law, but also gave us two new darling granddaughters to add to our collection. And recently, our daughter's best friend, whom we welcomed into our family years ago when she and my daughter were teenagers, came to see us to tell us that she and her husband are adopting a little girl. Now we have another granddaughter to look forward to welcoming into our family. The addition of these children into our family is a happy thing. Our lives are richer than we could have ever imagined.

In today's society, relationships can be shuffled and reshuffled, and even new marriages may dissolve and new relationships may form. Think of your own acquaintances who are on their third, fourth, or even fifth marriages. When worlds fall apart and are recreated, children often feel cast adrift. They need the stability that grandparents can give them.

According to the 2012 US Census Bureau statistics, over half of all marriages end in divorce, but that means that nearly half of all marriages stay together, making for all kinds of interesting relationships. Another statistic from the Census Bureau indicates that many divorced people, widows, and widowers remarry. In 2012, US Centers for Disease Control puts that number at 70–80 percent, depending on economics, race, and religion. It would seem reasonable to assume that many of those who remarry have parents of their own (us), which means it's more and more likely that at some point in our lives our children will put us in the position of being grandparents in some form or other.

Often we know how to do something because we've seen someone else do it, or at least heard stories about it. Stories of grandparents in fiction and reality shape how we behave as grandparents. Unfortunately, there aren't nearly as many stories about step-grandparents or non-traditional grandparents to help us out because the phenomenally high divorce rate is a fairly recent issue, leaving us with fewer stories to go on. We may feel like we are left floundering in an unknown sea with only the tiniest rudder to guide us.

However, this book gives us reason to rejoice. It is a collection of stories of real people who are making a success of being grandparents and grandchildren in many varied relationships and making a difference in their families. This book presents us with ideas that can help us map out our own course as we see how others have done it. From all the interviews I conducted for this book, I learned that there are certain principles that work. These principles include the time spent with grandchildren and the effort put into maintaining relationships, being non-judgmental, being there, and being loving, plus whatever variations on these principles that might be necessary or desirable at different times.

Another principle is humor—the kind that allows us to meet whatever circumstances that come along with grace, the kind that defuses an awkward moment, or the kind that softens a teaching moment. For instance, at the gym I overheard two elderly gentlemen discussing their grandchildren. The first grandfather said, "My grandson came to me and asked me to buy him a car." The second said, "What did you tell him?" The first said, "I told him that I'd be happy to buy him a car if he would make the monthly payments, buy the gas, and pay for the insurance." There was a pause before the second asked, "And what did he say to that?" The first said, "He said, 'Aw, Grandpa, I might as well buy the car myself.'" The two grandfathers laughed.

I am in awe of the extraordinary things people have done to benefit their families—things that they see as a normal part of their lives—even as I've become more grateful for the things my own grandparents did for me. In this book, we will meet some of these extraordinary people as they tell their own stories. At the end of the book are some short biographies about these people so you can get to know them and keep them straight as you read about them. I interviewed people who came from a variety of backgrounds, races, and cultures—from many regions of the United States as well as other countries—and found that the same principles hold true for nearly everyone. People are people all over the world. Each one of them had essentially the same things to say about the importance of time, effort, and attitude in maintaining relationships. As we read about how these people succeeded, my hope is to not only provide us with a rudder, but also the wind in our sails to set out with more confidence on that uncharted ocean called grandparenting.

Chapter One

Grandparents Can Save the World

It's true. Grandparents can save the world—or at least someone's world.

Throughout the years, grandparents meet with all kinds of joys and sorrows. Often, there are life tragedies that affect every person in the family to some degree and that are also part of living. Altered health, death, grief, legal concerns, visitation rights, loss of familiar surroundings, altered traditions and routines, changed familial relationships, finances—all have long-term repercussions on families. Grandparents can play a major role in bringing about stability, comfort, and even victory.

Grandparents have the power to be the anchors that keep the family ship from dashing on the rocks—for their own children and grandchildren, as well as the family members who have come into the family through marriage or adoption, legal or circumstantial.

Transition times are unsettling for everyone, but grandparents can be something solid to cling to.

Several of the people that I interviewed expressed the idea that when problems arise, grandparents can act as a cushion. As Sharon said, "After my father left us, my grandmother was a soft place to land." She was echoed by Leslie, who said, "With Grandma you have a safe place, because she'll never turn on you." Ellen added, "I am my grandson's safe place." Children need a place where they know they will receive unconditional love. That knowledge can give them the confidence to succeed and move forward with their lives. Knowing that they are loved alleviates anxiety and gives the family the strength to meet the challenges in their lives more successfully.

Ellen told about a book she read about displaced and abused children:

> I read that some kids succumb to the unfortunate circumstances and repeat the past, but others come out strong, and the ones who do have at least one normal relationship where they feel loved and safe. It might be a long-distance aunt or someone at church or someone outside of their day-to-day lives. If just an occasional relationship that is a special relationship can help a child in a terribly abusive situation, imagine what I can do for my grandson who is loved. He is still going to know that I am there when I can be, and that will help him.

As I interviewed people, I found that nearly everyone had stories of how the love and attention of a grandparent or interaction with grandchildren made life better, and their experiences often contained elements of things I could do to strengthen my own grandparenting relationships.

For example, Ellen also said,

> When I was growing up, I had an alcoholic stepfather and all the shouting and arguing that came with it. My grandma's house was the normal house. It was where I was loved unconditionally and where I knew there would always be clean sheets and cookies. You couldn't count on that at my house. My folks smoked and the first few minutes we were at Grandma's we washed ourselves, our hair, and our clothes so we felt clean and comfortable. That sense of normalcy and safety is what I need to be for my grandchildren.

It is important to note that she aspires to be the type of grandmother she is because of her own grandmother, who gave her a benchmark to aim for. Because of what she learned from her grandmother, future generations are blessed. This is a common theme throughout this book and what people had to say when I interviewed them.

For example, Mitzi said,

> I was in an abusive relationship before Dick and I married. Dick is so good to us and his children and my children and his grandchildren and my grandchildren. We all feel that our families got to have the parenting they didn't have before. Our children saw how much we were in love and they wanted that so much. My children so appreciate what Dick has done for me, and his children feel so glad that we are together and what we did for the other one that they want that. Even the grandchildren see

what we have and they want it. They see our example and it makes them want the same kind of marriage. We were in love when we got married, and it wasn't for convenience like some second marriages, so that was a security for the kids and we still do have that love for each other. The kids say they want a marriage like ours. We tell them that you have the choice of what kind of marriage you have and you can all have it if you want.

So, just being a good example can benefit the family. The stability of a good marriage can have benefits for generations.

For Lily's family, her step-grandfather made the difference between poverty and financial stability after her father abandoned Lily and her mother. Life would have been much different if her grandfather had not been there to help pick up the pieces. The result is that Lily has a college degree, a successful career, a good marriage, and three darling children. Future generations feel the effects of good grandparenting.

All of the people interviewed for this book told of the things they've done to change their families, and if I'd had time to interview more, I would have found many other extraordinary stories, because grandparents everywhere are making a difference. For example, after their son's remarriage, Tom and Deirdre found that taking a volatile teenage grandson into their home for a weekend visit could help defuse conflict, while also cementing the bond between them and the grandson.

My own grandparents had me visit them every summer, took me shopping—complete with a traditional stop to buy hot fudge sundaes and scones—and provided me with a small stipend while I went to college. My own step-grandmother was a kind, gentle lady who provided delicious meals and comfortable evenings as the family sang around the piano. My own parents were stricken with polio when I was a small child, and my sister and I were farmed out to relatives until my parents, although crippled by the disease, were able to take care of us again. My grandparents helped me feel like I had a normal childhood, even though our family went through several rough patches.

Similarly, Cathy remembers staying with her grandmother every weekend for several years, which helped her avoid combative situations at home and made her teenage years happy ones. She said, "I liked spending time at my grandma's house because it was peaceful. We'd ride the metro bus and we'd go shopping. We'd go visiting aunts and other people. Then I'd go home on Sunday." Cathy added that, because of her grandmother's example, she wants to be like her when she has grandchildren. She said, "I'm going to try to be as self-sufficient as I can. I want to take care of the kids as much as possible. I'd love to be an Auntie Mame, but I won't have the means. But I'll be here." Cathy's grandchildren will benefit because of what a woman three generations distant did for their own grandmother.

Leslie also wants to be like her grandmother. Like Cathy, she was a little girl with a less-than-desirable family situation. Leslie's grandmother made all the difference in her life. She said,

> I think that because she thought I was wonderful and could do no wrong she helped my self-esteem. It didn't matter if my parents were mad at me because I knew that Grandma loved me. When things got bad, I used to make up little vacations to visit her. I would go on these little vacations to her house for a few days at a time. She took me to Woolworth's and I could pick a toy for a dollar. Little things like that made me feel like I was on top of the world.

The mention of little things is significant. Notice that it did not take a lot of money to make either Leslie or Cathy feel wanted. Their grandmothers gave them a place of refuge, kind words of encouragement and praise, a ride on a bus, or a dollar to spend. Yet it was these little things that are remembered and appreciated.

The qualities of grandparenting sometimes need to be employed in situations that are unexpected. When their daughter Tiffany was a child, Angela and Mitch took Tiffany's best friend, Brenda, into their family. Brenda had a difficult family life, so she spent most of her time living with them. Angela said,

> Tiffany often begged, "Can't we adopt her?" I told her that Brenda had a family with a mother and father and brothers and sisters, and then Tiffany would say, "But they don't want her. Can't we adopt her?" I had to admit that they didn't. So, although we couldn't adopt her, we let Brenda stay with us most of the time. She is one of our family. Later, when Brenda's marriage fell apart, she brought her kids to live with us.

Brenda's children consider Angela and Mitch to be their grandparents even though there are no blood ties. Angela said,

> The oldest girl resents us for making it so her mother could leave her father, but the other two were much happier living with us. The boy, Josh, once told his older sister that I was her real grandmother—that none of their other grandmothers would do for them what I had done. When I went to the kid's games, I was often introduced as Brenda's mother. I asked them what if one of the real grandmothers showed up and they said there was no chance of that

happening. Now that they are grown up and two of them have children of their own, I am still invited to family parties and am considered the grandma.

The important point of Angela and Mitch's story is that their willingness to include others in their family, even those not related to them, has benefited generations of Brenda's family and also enriched Angela and Mitch's life, as we will see in another chapter. Additionally, Angela's efforts to go to her "adopted" grandchildren's games and take an interest in their activities, cemented their relationship.

Many grandparents end up raising their grandchildren for one reason or another. Raising a grandchild can be a huge commitment—financially and emotionally—but many grandparents still do it. For example, Roslyn and Stephen's son divorced and his wife took their grandson, Tim, to another state. The ex-wife let Tim come to visit Roslyn and Stephen every summer for a few weeks. Roslyn said,

> One summer she called and asked if we would keep Tim here. She was not very nice about it. She always needed more money from our son and from us. When we asked her why, she said I owe so much money all over the place and I have to have a second job. So we said that would be fine. We would be happy to have Tim come live with us. Then we said that we've been sending you child support, so you should help pay for his expenses. We never saw a penny all those years from when he was twelve to his final year of high school, but we were glad to take care of him.

Having grandparents who were glad to take care of him probably did a lot to help the boy feel that he is wanted, especially when his life turned upside down.

Raising Tim wasn't the end of raising their grandchildren. One of their daughters developed an emotional illness, made worse by her verbally abusive and controlling husband. She moved in with Roslyn and Stephen. Later, even when their daughter was able to get a place of her own, the oldest granddaughter, Jennie, continued staying with Roslyn and Stephen until she graduated from high school, and eventually her younger sister, Charlotte, joined her. Roslyn said,

> It didn't take very long until the little one started school and needed to be picked up and what have you, so we would pick Charlotte up and take her home. Then our daughter got remarried and that was that for Charlotte. With her new marriage, our daughter didn't want Charlotte all the time. We had to take her, too. We had Charlotte for ten years.

By taking in their grandchildren, Roslyn and Stephen gave them stability and opportunities they might not have had while their mother wrestled with emotional illness. Their efforts paid off. Both girls have made successes of their lives.

Roslyn and Stephen are proud of their grandchildren and their accomplishments. Roslyn said,

> Jennie finished high school when she was sixteen and went to the university for a year, and then she joined the National Guard and she went to boot camp and to Monterey to the language school and studied Farsi. After she was married, she got deployed to Iraq for a year and she was an interrogator. She worked with an Iraqi who translated for her. She came back and worked for a school in Arizona teaching interrogating, and after a year-and-a-half her husband was accepted to law school in Washington DC. She now

works for the Pentagon. There is a possibility that she would be deployed again. She is in law school now. We're very proud of her.

The younger one is also on a good path. Roslyn said, "Now Charlotte is in college. Somehow we will have to find the money. Charlotte is just the best and she does so well. We keep in touch with her mother. Her mother comes over for Sunday dinner to be with us."

When asked how he felt about taking in his grandchildren, Stephen said,

> It came as natural as possible. When I hear about grandparents who don't want to see their grandchildren, I can't believe them. They are part of our family. That was a given. Our doors were open when we were needed. We just flowed with it. Remember, Abraham had his sons and children live with him. It was just like that but we didn't live in a tent.

Notice that Roslyn and Stephen stepped in when they had to, meeting the needs of their grandchildren while maintaining a relationship with their own daughter. It probably wasn't always easy, yet Stephen said it was "as natural as possible." Also of importance is the fact that while Roslyn and Stephen have not stopped being providers of comfort and support, they also let Jennie and Charlotte choose their own course and are proud of their accomplishments.

The role of a grandparent or step-grandparent is a powerful one, because of the influence that can be had on the grandchildren. Several years ago, I had a student who had been placed in foster care. Through comments he made in class over the course of the year, he demonstrated over and over again that he was pretty well grounded. He often came up with answers to questions that other students didn't know. We had a few conversations after class where he told me of some of the conflict that had happened in his family, such as abuse, divorce, and foster care, as well as how much he hated his father. He also told me that he had ended up in foster care after his grandfather had died, because his grandfather had been the only safety net he'd had within his family. One day, he said something in class that was very wise. I asked him where he learned something so valuable. He said he learned it from his grandfather. Later, I asked, "Gene, why would you listen to your grandfather, when you wouldn't listen to your father?" Gene said, "Because he said it in a grandfatherly sort of way."

A grandfatherly sort of way—what does that mean and why would it be received differently from something a parent or stepparent might say? For one thing, a grandparent is not always the disciplinarian. Grandparents are not often involved in the daily grind of urging children to do chores or get to school or go to bed, even if they are a caregiver. Grandchildren may even behave better for grandparents. As one grandchild put it, "I know I have to behave because my grandparents don't have to put up with me. They can send me back at any time."

A grandparent or step-grandparent can be in the privileged position of being the non-judgmental listener, the one who provides pleasant experiences, the person who loves unconditionally. As Christopher put it, "The joy of grandparenting in a blended family is that the grandparent is non-judgmental and can help smooth difficult situations with the child. I don't think the grandparent is good at smoothing things over with the parents because there is too much baggage there. But with the child, he or she can empathize and counsel."

Bethany agrees. She said, "After my divorce, my children's grandparents were important. Because they were really involved and had always been very involved, the children loved being with them. That gave them security and someone to talk to because grandparents don't have the same sets of rules as the parents."

Both Bethany and Christopher recognized the unique place grandparents have. The important thing is that the grandparents made the effort to be there when they were needed and were a stable influence.

Effort is a huge factor in establishing stable and worthwhile relationships with grandchildren. Many of the grandparents whom I interviewed told of events they consciously planned in order to develop relationships with family members. Others told about the many efforts their grandparents made for them. These events took time and work, but they were worth it in the long run and had repercussions that span generations.

For example, Stan and Dolores loved to have the family over for barbecues, holiday, and birthday parties. These get-togethers, along with lots of good food, helped the stepfamily interact with each other and gradually develop friendships that made family relations more comfortable. "Family solidarity was our goal," said Dolores. "It was a goal I got from my parents who got it from my grandfather. He actually published a little pamphlet on family solidarity to encourage his descendants to stick together."

One of Stan's biggest successes is his traditional Valentine's Day party. "Every year, the family looks forward to my party that I put on by myself. I got the idea from my father-in-law who planned a similar type of party and even put up his own decorations and got the refreshments himself," he said. Stan goes to a lot of work for weeks before his party. He sets up tables with different games and contests for his family to play in small groups. He also makes up a schedule so the groups rotate and change members every fifteen minutes. Each person has a score card made especially for him or her. At the end of the evening, just before the food is brought out, the family gathers to add up scores. Stan makes up categories of winners that include each person so he can give prizes to everyone, such as stuffed animals, action figures, and other toys, perfumes, gadgets, and jewelry. Everyone is a winner. Everyone laughs and has a good time and looks forward to the next year. "We're a family, and my party helps us get to know each other better so we feel like a family with fond memories of each other," said Stan.

Building memories is extremely important and can help smooth over many rough spots in the lives of children. The efforts don't have to be huge. They can take the form of just offering support or taking an interest in what grandchildren do. Myfanwy said,

> My grandparents were a big part of my life and I loved them. And still do. They gave me a lot of attention and taught me a lot of things and gave me a lot of great opportunities, especially when I was really sick as a child for long periods of time. And they were, for the most part, really supportive. Grandma and Grandpa are always happy for us to come over and sing to them and play the piano. That is a safe place for us to gain some confidence in our musical abilities.

Notice that she didn't mention expensive presents or grand vacations as her fondest memories. She remembers the times her grandparents took care of her when she was ill and also the interest they took in her talents. The care that her grandparents had for her was important to her and made a difference in her life.

However, her husband, Sean, had a very different experience with his step-grandfather:

> He's kind of an interesting guy. He's sort of taciturn. The first time I met him was when my Grandma and he took me out to dinner once when I was in college. So I talked to him there a little bit. That was the first time I remember him. But then I found out he was

> a friend of the family and had been for a long time. My mom and grandmother and aunt knew him in the Philippines before they moved here. My grandma has never really shown that much interest when we were around. She mostly just sits on a couch and reads a book or sleeps and doesn't really talk to us that much. I think it's related to how she doesn't get along with my mom that well.

Notice that his grandmother's behavior made Sean aware of family tension.

Myfanwy and Sean's very different experiences point out a major principle that became apparent during the interviews for this book: children blossom when grandparents take the time and put in the effort to pay attention to them. However, lack of attention makes grandchildren insecure about relationships or even aware of difficulties in the family. This feeling of insecurity can make them unsure about other things in their lives as well.

On the opposite end of the spectrum, Tom and Deirdre put their own personal stamp on being grandparents. Tom has always taken his grandchildren on individual outings from the time they could walk, so it seemed natural to give the new step-grandchildren their own outings with Papa. Tom said, "The child can choose the activity, such as going to a movie, playing miniature golf, or going out to dinner, something like that, and it is something they look forward to a lot, and I do, too."

In fact, Tom said that "Papa Time" is one of the delights his natural grandchildren promised their new stepsiblings when they joined the family. Now the step-grandchildren ask as eagerly as the grandchildren when their next Papa Time will be.

While Tom has Papa Time, Deirdre loves sports and has season tickets to football and basketball games at the local university. Since Tom isn't interested in going, she takes a grandchild or step-grandchild with her to games. She said, "We've developed a ritual of arriving early enough to eat some traditional game food, such as hot dogs and ice cream before going to our seats, and the kids look forward to it. They know we have to cheer really loud, too. They know what we're going to do and that we're going to have fun."

Traditions have helped create a bond between Tom and Deirdre and their grandchildren. Both Tom and Deirdre find that the time driving to and from events and while they are waiting for things to start present opportunities for their grandchildren and step-grandchildren to chatter away about their lives or unload their problems. If a child is quiet, a few questions usually loosen his or her tongue. Tom and Deirdre have also learned not to get into the middle of familial conflict and to offer only sympathy, not judgments. As Deirdre said, "Being judgmental is death."

Ellen did not really look forward to being a grandparent, but she surprised herself when she became one. She said,

> When my oldest grandson was born, I was in the delivery room. My daughter had these huge expectations of me being a doting grandmother who would go crazy over my grandchild. I am not a baby person. I mean, I like children, but I don't care that much about just being with any children. But from the first time I saw my grandson as he was being born, I have become a super-grandma, and I do go crazy over him. I believe that God puts special relationships between generations for a reason—that there is a place for grandparents with their grandchildren. I see so many opportunities to correct mistakes I made with my children with my grandchildren. It places almost a burden on me. But I really love that little guy.

Caleb has no grandchildren of his own and considers his step-grandchildren as his own. He said, "To anyone who tries to say that my grandchildren are step-grandchildren, I always say there is no step between me and my grandchildren." While discussing how he built such a close bond with them, he said, "I learned along the way that I get to define the relationship with the grandchildren. I'm the adult, so I get to decide how we interact." That's an important point. As grandparents, we are the adults, and we get to decide about how we interact with our grandchildren.

Early in his second marriage, Caleb decided to be directly involved in his step-grandchildren's lives. He is a journalist who can work from home, so he has the opportunity to be with the children on a daily basis, especially since he is often the caregiver while his wife and stepchildren work, so he involves the children as he conducts interviews, works in his garden, or does chores. He helps them with their homework and even pays half of their tuition to private schools.

Caleb was thrust into the role of step-grandparent soon after his marriage to his second wife when his stepdaughter became pregnant and split up with her boyfriend. He said,

> Xander's biological father was not part of his life for the first few years, but now they are married and on their third child. I was his parent as he grew up, and still to this day I sit down and do his homework with him. I taught him to read, and I cleaned up his vomit and changed his diapers. We have a bond that defines our lives.

Christopher agrees with Caleb about the importance of bonding with step-grandchildren. He said,

> Regardless of the blood relationship, or lack thereof, I have found that if grandparents of blended families

work to earn trust, to love, and to participate in the lives of the children, neither the grandparent nor the child considers the word step. They love and protect equally. In many cases, if the step-grandparent engages more than the blood grandparent, there is a greater bond. So, grandparenting has little to do with blood and much to do with engagement.

Christopher's mother and stepfather, Ann and Ed, have had a huge influence on their grandchildren. Ann said,

> Ed is an extremely unusual man who has a great love for people. When I die, there are going to be a lot of women on my front porch wanting to marry him. Both of us had close families, and we kind of carried that over to ours. Once you have that kind of relationship and you carry it over to your family, it can carry on with the grandchildren. It started when Ed and I were dating. He got along so well with Christopher that one time when he was out front fixing the water pump, Christopher jumped on his back and said, "Are you going to marry my Mom?" I don't know what Ed said, but we eventually got married and Ed made a huge difference in our lives.

Ed added,

> I met Christopher when I started dating his mother. He was seven years old. I always like to be punctual, and his mother wasn't always ready, so I played with him until she was ready. It was winter time and so we were in the house. We kind of wrassled and he kept after me to play with him. He needed a little friendship or something. Come spring, he wanted a kite

and so I got the funny papers and made a kite and we entered a contest and whoever could get the highest kite got the prize. We got the kite so high it broke the string and we didn't win anything. It was a good kite. It sailed really good. When I was a boy we made things or we didn't have them. I also made him a couple of Pinewood Derby cars. It was that kind of relationship that we carried over to the grandchildren.

Ann added,

> Before we were married, he just took the place of a father. For example, we went down to Lake Powell before we were married, and Christopher wanted a water ski merit badge. He had to go off a dock and land on his skis, but he was scared. I remember him looking all white and shivery, but determined to do it. Ed had to show him how to do it, and he did. Ed just taught him about things. He taught him about pigeons and how to raise chickens and rabbits. He taught him things that he knew as a boy, which was when he lived in St. George out on a farm. Ed taught him lots of things other boys didn't know how to do. They went winter camping in the snow. He showed him how to saddle and bridle a horse. Ed taught him how to shoot. They had a great time together. Christopher thought of him as more of a father than his own father, and that relationship is what Ed has with Christopher's children.

Not only time and effort are vital in the bonding process between children and adults. It is also important to be inclusive, to extend the influence of grandparents to all the children, so that interaction with them is a natural result of a normal relationship.

Diane and Randy have several grandchildren, but the oldest, Riley, was placed in a difficult position when his father, Diane and Randy's son, committed suicide. After a while, Riley's mother remarried and had other children, which presented a unique opportunity to Diane and Randy. Diane said,

> After our son died and his wife remarried, we would go see Riley. When we went to pick him up, his little half-sister Emma would run to the door saying, "Grandma, Grandma, Grandma." She didn't understand that we weren't her grandparents, just Riley's. She was so little it just was hard not to hurt this little girl, so I told her mother at the time when we took Riley that Emma was welcome to come, too. We talked to Emma's father about it. I didn't want her own father to feel weird about it, but he was very open to us. We became attached to Emma. At Christmas and birthdays it seemed odd to give one a gift and not the other, so we give her presents, too.

Diane and Randy's other children have joined with them in welcoming Emma into their family. Their daughter, Ashley, said, "I adopted Emma, too, and it was my parents' example that made us do the same. We weren't sure if that would be awkward at first, so we just did it. Like my mother said, 'How can you cut a little girl off?' So, I buy her birthday presents and Christmas presents just like I do for Riley." Notice that Diane and Randy's attitude toward Emma encouraged a similar attitude in their daughter, which, in turn, benefited Emma further.

Circumstances changed, and Riley and Emma's family moved to a different state, but Diane and Randy try to write letters and call to maintain their relationship. They feel that what could have been an awkward situation ended up enriching their lives. Additionally,

Diane and Randy's example of kindness encouraged their own children to be kind to a little girl who really had no blood claim on them. That culture of kindness will have repercussions for the whole family.

～

Besides working to be good grandparents, several people I interviewed told of how much they appreciated their own grandparents who helped them through difficult situations—how their grandparents helped to save their worlds. For example, Cari said, "I would call my grandma if my mom wasn't listening because she always answered the phone and had good ears along with some good advice." Cari's grandmother was that reliable and soft place to land mentioned by Sharon and Leslie.

Melanie also valued her grandmother, especially after her mother remarried. She appreciated the time her grandmother took to reassure her, because, as she said, "I was so worried at age ten, when I found out about my mother remarrying. I hated the guy." Her grandmother often invited Melanie and her brothers and sisters to stay with her on her farm. She provided stability for her grandchildren in an uncertain time, and she gave them a good example that wasn't provided in their nuclear family. Melanie said, "My grandmother was well-read and had books that covered the large living room wall. She loved her *Time* magazine and kept current on politics. She read poems to us, talked about planting, harvesting, the weather, etc. My Gram always had the right answer for whatever my question was."

Lily remembers the efforts her step-grandparents made to bond with her. They were a huge part of her life. For example, she said,

> On my fourteenth birthday, just my grandparents, including my step-grandpa, on my mom's side, were

there and they made it really special. Now, my stepdad's mom always makes me birthday dinner. My other grandpa always helped me with my homework. My stepdad's parents are really young, in their 60s, and we go four-wheeling with them and do fun things. My step-grandpa is the cook in that family. He makes good omelets. He's a four-wheeler guy. He has a column every week about four-wheeling. I used to edit them for him, but he's passed me up. Between my mom's side and my stepdad's side, there are all kinds of relationships. There's no talk about half-brothers or stepsisters or in-laws. We're not always happy, but we're a family.

Family—that's what it's all about, isn't it? And grandparents can help a family be a family.

Chapter Two

Meet the New Family

Is It Love, Hate, Terror, or Indifference at First Sight and Beyond?

At a hotel where I was staying, I witnessed a tender situation that was probably the meeting of a grandparent and his granddaughter for the first time in a long time, or even the first time ever. I was in the hotel hot tub when a very pretty young woman came into the pool area carrying a little girl about three years old. The little girl's stiffness and the way she held herself away from the woman indicated that she felt like she was in an alien place and was unsure of what was happening. I wondered if she was afraid of the water. Even when the woman stepped down into the hot tub and deposited her on the edge, the little girl didn't cling to the woman who was holding her or even speak to her. She was just afraid.

A few minutes later, a young man joined them in the hot tub. The little girl immediately cuddled up to him, and I got the impression that he was her father. From the conversation between the young man and the young woman, I figured out that she was his girlfriend. I got that impression because he told her things about the little girl, like when her birthday was and what she liked to eat, and that made me think this was the first time the girlfriend had either met the little girl or had much to do with her. No wonder the little girl was uneasy with the young woman.

The story became more complicated when a middle-aged man joined them. The young man seemed very happy to see the older man. He said to the little girl, "Here's Papa! Here's Papa!" He was excited for his daughter to meet her grandfather. The little girl clearly had no idea who this older man was, and her face was expressionless as she shrank against her father, but her father seemed to expect her to know that meeting Papa was a wonderful thing. It was in his voice and body language.

Since we were all in the hot tub together, it was hard not to hear what was being said. Through the rest of the conversation, I got the impression that this family was meeting at a hotel as neutral ground so they could get to know each other. I was impressed that Papa gently asked questions of both the little girl and his son's girlfriend without pushing and that he was interested in them without needing to talk about himself. As soon as I could gracefully exit the hot tub, I left so they could have some privacy.

Later, I saw them walking around the hotel grounds. The young man and young woman were holding hands, and Papa had the little girl on his shoulders as they walked behind her father and his girlfriend. The little girl was chattering away. She had her arms wrapped around Papa's head, which he seemed to find delightful. Evidently Papa's gentleness and the fact that they were on neutral ground was working. I thought that their family was on the way to building a good relationship.

As I interviewed people about meeting their new steprelatives, it became evident that Papa's method of gentle inquiry and interest was an important strategy in building what will be a lifelong relationship. From his own experience as a stepson and step-grandson, Christopher said, "Treat them like you would any new child. Get on their level, and earn their trust."

Christopher's stepmother, Mitzi, said,

> It's harder to merge a family when both parents are alive. It's a little harder. You have to be more careful because those children still have feelings for their other parents and grandparents. So you have to be careful to not insist that they think of you as their parents or grandparents, but you can do things to make it easier.

She added,

> Meeting Christopher was the hardest one of all because he lived with his mother. It was very confusing for him to come over here and have fun. He would start having fun, and then I'd see him, and he would get quiet. To make it easy for him, I said, "I'm not trying to be your mother. I'm just being your father's wife," and he had to think about that. We took him to church with us and things like that. He said he remembered that I always sat and stroked his arm to keep him quiet. Touch helped, and in that situation he could allow it, and in other situations he probably couldn't.

Sharon, whose children have two sets of step-grandparents, agrees that the way adults meet new children in their lives is important. She advises new step-grandparents to "be welcoming, and take an interest in them without overwhelming them." It is important to remember that, even if you are uncomfortable, the children are pretty much at the mercy of what their parents have decided will happen for their family and need the reassurance of the adults as everyone negotiates new territory.

For example, Mitzi said,

> I know people think that what is different between your children and stepchildren is that you don't have time to bond. When the step-grandchildren came along, it was the parents that allowed us to bond like they were our own. I don't think that the grandchildren think of me any different. I had a friend who told me she told her children that she already raised her children, and she expects her children to raise their children, and she doesn't want them to think she wants to be involved. I can't believe anyone would feel that way, unless you don't like children. I love all the grandchildren and love being involved with them.

Mitzi made an important point—it is the parents who allow the grandparents to have a relationship with their grandchildren. Parents are the gatekeepers, which is why it is so important for parents and grandparents to make the effort to get along. Otherwise, grandchildren may not have the opportunity to know their grandparents.

Deirdre said,

> At the back of my mind, when we met our son's new girlfriend and her children, was that everyone present was bringing different baggage to the meeting. I certainly knew of the hurt and rage my own grandchildren still felt over their mother walking out on them, even though it was a year ago. I knew the new girlfriend's ex-husband had left her, too, so everyone had abandonment issues. Yet, here we were trying

to be polite and cheerful as we met her and her children. I wanted things to go well for my son's sake. He was so hopeful, and I was grateful to this woman for giving him hope, and I also wanted to establish our relationship with her and her children from the first.

Tom said, "I was eager to love them. I wanted to love them like my own grandchildren, just as if they were born into my family and I held them in my arms from the beginning. No judgment. I wanted to love them on their own terms."

The first meeting was made easier for them by their son inviting his parents over to his house. His girlfriend and her children were already comfortable with his own family and had been to his house several times, so when Tom and Deirdre walked in, it was to a family party that was already in motion. The natural grandchildren ran to hug Tom and Deirdre and tell them their news. Deirdre said, "Introductions were made in the middle of all this commotion, and everyone fell into friendly conversation. In subsequent meetings, the girlfriend's children were included in the grandparent hugging and a pattern of loving goodwill was established. That first meeting kind of set the stage for how we all interact now."

Bethany also offers good advice:

> You have to take yourself out of the equation, and you have to place yourself in a position so you don't make your step-grandchildren uncomfortable. Don't be aggressive. Don't rush in and just pick them up and say "I'm your grandparent, and you have to love me." That's offensive. Instead, be loving toward them, and let them set the pace. The focus is on them rather than on yourself.

She feels that a new step-grandparent can avoid problems with careful planning. She said,

A pitfall is becoming too possessive and having your feelings hurt and having you wonder if they love you, rather than turning it around and loving them no matter what. Otherwise there is too much jealousy and competition. You have to take yourself out of the equation and put yourself in the part where you are more concerned with them than yourself. Sometimes they will be concerned that they will be disloyal to their own family if they love you. I think it's more prevalent in step situations through divorce or death. The kids are so emotional about that, so standing your ground and saying they're your grandchildren is a pitfall.

Stan and Dolores had an uncomfortable first encounter with their new step-grandchildren, even though they had good intentions. Their future son-in-law was from a different state, but his children lived with their mother, his ex-wife, not far from Stan and Dolores. That meant that the initial meeting had to be at Stan and Dolores's house and that the children were brought over from their mother's house by their father.

"We wanted to love the children, but they came in the front door like scared rabbits," Dolores said. "While the adults sat on the couches, the children sat in a huddle on the floor."

Stan said, "I tried to draw them out with questions, but it felt more like the Inquisition. It took years for them to warm up to us, but even though things got better as they got older, they always kept us at a distance."

"It was unfortunate," Dolores said. "Eventually, we gave up on putting them on the same level with our natural grandchildren because they made it clear they didn't want it that way."

Stan said, "Looking back on it, we would have been wiser to meet them at some neutral place, like a park or something, although things are a little easier now because we invite them to parties where they can mingle with the rest of the family, and the focus isn't on them."

Overcoming awkwardness takes courage and continuous effort. As Caleb said, "I learned along the way that I get to define the relationship with the grandchildren. There were a lot of times when no one was willing to step forward. It takes some confidence to throw yourself into this situation." He added, "I think it's important that the kids feel they're loved and accepted. An attitude of love and acceptance certainly makes it easier."

From an adopted child's perspective, Julie said,

> I came into the family at the age of five. And it was hard for me to accept all the family at once, but my grandmothers [including a step-grandmother] loved me unconditionally and won my heart—each in her own unique way. As the step-grandchild, however, I would say hugs galore, kisses on the cheek and forehead whenever they are around. Let them know they are unique individuals and wanted as a member of the family. Introduce them to everyone as your newest grandchild and say how delighted you are that they have joined the family.

Wanting the children and being delighted to have them makes all the difference in how the family accepts them and how they accept you.

I have also found that the way I introduce my grandchildren and step-grandchildren makes a difference to them. I try to put that delight into my voice so they know I love them and am proud of them. They don't say much about how I do introductions, but their expressions show that they feel reassured about my feelings toward them every time. Children can sense if an adult is delighted to know them and accepts them.

Christopher appreciated the time and effort his stepfather put into their relationship and how that foundation has influenced his own children:

> I was a trusting soul who thought if you're the head of the family you should love everybody because of my stepfather who was a really good guy with me. So my own children have that expectation, and as far as they're concerned, he is their grandfather. He spent time with me, one-on-one time with things I wanted to do. I remember flying a kite together, going to Lake Powell, and riding horses. You have to be willing to cut each other some slack while building a relationship of trust. You invite and commit. It has to be sincere. Stepparents and step-grandparents themselves have to be the first initiators and have to build that relationship with the child.

Christopher's mother and stepfather, Ann and Ed, do many things to make their grandchildren feel more comfortable with them. Ann said,

> Ask them what they want to do with their lives and what their goals are. Ask them about school. Interact with the child. Play games with them. We'd always play Chinese checkers and other games. We take them on trips and such. Tell them stories of when you were a child. Get them interested in when you were a child. Ed is a great storyteller, and the children are always asking him to tell them this or that story.

So it would seem that not only time and effort are important for step-grandparents to develop family relationships with step-grandchildren, but also an attitude of inclusion and delight. Children want to be loved and accepted and will usually respond positively to such treatment, often with effects that last generations. Julie, who was adopted, said her adopted grandparents influenced how she treats her own grandchildren: "I give them unquestioning approval—that is what my grandmothers gave me and my mother gave my children and I give my grandchildren. That is a must to nurturing healthy children into responsible adults. They never question if they are loved or approved of by Grammie and Papo."

Bethany added,

> I think the key to grandparenting, and there is one more step with step-grandchildren with unpleasant circumstances that leads you to this place, is that you have to think of the children and step back and have a consistent relationship with the child. The whole point is the happiness of the children."

I would add that if the children are happy, it is more likely that you as a grandparent will be happy, too.

Leslie said that with her new grandchildren, she was compared to the existing grandparents. She said,

> With two sets of my grandchildren, there is the other grandma and the good grandma. The others yell at them or criticize, but I never do. I started taking the oldest girl out when my son and his new wife had a new baby. It was obvious there were some hard feelings there. The oldest girl resented the new baby. So every Thursday we went to McDonald's and did other things. We also made cookies. I think it made a difference to her and her mom and her baby sister. I took pictures of our outings every week so she'll remember when I'm dead and gone that I did that for her.

Leslie was aware that there could be difficulties in a new marriage when a baby comes and there are existing children. That awareness was not the end of it, though. Leslie also acted to smooth over a rough spot. She gave her granddaughter the kind of attention that told her she was loved as much as the new baby, and she took pictures of their outing to reinforce her love.

One of the big questions that arises with the convoluted relationships formed through remarriage is how to resolve relationships with the grandchildren's step- or half-siblings and the extended family on the other side. Diane and Randy handled the situation with their grandson's half-sister very well, but they didn't just fall into the relationship. Diane said, "My husband Randy and I had to talk about it for a long time. If we continued this relationship with Emma, it meant a commitment that we would have to take on for years. Like I said, we couldn't hurt this little girl, so we did it."

Diane and Randy's commitment was also a commitment for the whole family. Ashley, their daughter, said,

> My parents are compassionate people, so I know they were concerned for Emma. Their relationship with her meant my sisters and I were considered Emma's aunts. I buy her birthday presents and Christmas presents and treat her like she is my own niece and she comes to family birthday parties with all the kids. My other siblings also buy her presents and include her, not as much as I do, but it's a commitment for our whole family.

Notice that the compassion of the grandparents rubbed off on the rest of the family.

On the other hand, grandparents are always meeting new people that come into their families—even when they are blood relations. Every new baby is a new personality to add to the mix. Grandparents have to establish relationships with these infant newcomers, as well as people who come into the family in other ways. Often the relationships grow and change over the years as the grandchildren grow and change, but with babies it all starts with a birth announcement.

For example, many years ago a woman I worked with got a call from her son while she was at her desk not far from mine. She shrieked with joy when she heard that she was going to be a grandmother. When she hung up the phone, she leaped up and danced down the hall, singing loudly as she told everyone in the building her good news. Everybody laughed. I thought they were laughing because she was being silly in a very public way, although I'm sure some of them were just happy for her. But at that time, in all my inexperience, I was embarrassed for her and vowed never to behave in such a juvenile manner when I had grandchildren.

That was then.

This is what happened to me: I remember feeling happy when I found out that my oldest son and his wife were going to have a baby. However, I was determined not to be silly about it, like my co-worker. Several weeks later, my son and his wife asked me to come with them when they had the ultrasound, so I went. I was unprepared for what happened to my heart when I saw my grandson's perfect little profile so clearly on the screen. My heart welled up inside me, and it was all I could do not to sing or dance, just like my co-worker. Somehow I managed to contain my feelings. I walked my son and his wife out to their car and waved good-bye in a dignified way, but as soon as their car was out of the parking lot, I jumped up and down and screamed and laughed and cried and danced all over the parking lot. Luckily no one was around. Then I drove to the store and bought little footballs and boy clothes for my grandson.

My co-worker and I are not alone in our reactions to becoming grandparents. As Ellen said in the last chapter, she had a crazy reaction when she saw her first grandson being born. It was with her son's son, the second grandson, that she lost it in public. She said,

> When I found out he was a boy, my husband and I were in Disney World in the middle of the Disney Store, and I shouted, 'It's a boy! It's a boy!' and held out my cell phone as if everyone could see. Then I bought a million dollars worth of stuff— little boy clothes and little boy this and that. Everyone stared at me, and I'm sure I embarrassed my husband.

Ellen realized with the second one that her relationship with her son's family living a thousand miles away would be different from her relationship with her daughter's family, living a few minutes away. She said,

> Now one lives nearby, and the other is far away. I was so concerned because I have such a special relationship with the first, and there are differences between a son's baby and a daughter's baby. When I think of my grandson in Kentucky, it breaks my heart because I can't pick him up from the babysitter or take him on outings or visit on a daily basis. I was there when he was born, but I had to go home for six weeks. When I went back for a visit, he had grown and morphed, and it broke my heart. How can I be there for both of them? How do I do that when they are 2,000 miles apart? I decided that all you can do is love them and be yourself. I keep looking at a book I read that said all they need is one strong example and one loving relationship with an adult to grow

up to be strong and successful. Hopefully I can be an impact that way.

Influencing and impacting are a natural part of grandparents interacting with their grandchildren. Children can't help but see how the adults in their lives behave, succeed, fail, or proceed through life. Grandparents can give children a solid foundation to stand on through example, as well as love and support.

Chapter Three

What Do They Call You?

How Many Grandmas Are There?

In today's society, especially with the high rate of divorce and remarriage, we are presented with an astonishing array of family relationships. All of those relations have to be called something, if only for clarity.

When I was a child, kinship terms were simplified for me on my mother's side as all adult males, except my blood grandparents, were called "Uncle" and adult females were called "Aunt." It wasn't until I was an adult that I found that some were cousins, some were steps, and some really were my aunts and uncles or great-aunts and uncles. But at least I knew what to call them. There was no confusion there, and everyone seemed happy with the arrangement. Knowing what to call family members is important.

Lily's family is large, and relations are complicated, but somehow they have all been sorted out satisfactorily. Lily said, "My real grandpa had two children, and then grandmother divorced him. My step-grandfather had three children, and they all called the grandpas 'Daddy.' In our family, there is no talk about half-brothers or stepsisters or in-laws."

When Bethany married into her new family, her step-grandchildren had to decide what to call her. She said,

> The grandchildren call me "Grandma Bethany" (Grandma B) because there are too many grandmas — at least four grandmas per child. They say "That's the grandma with the curly hair" or "That's the grandma who lives in that place." They had a hard time telling us apart until they figured out they could call me "Grandma B." My husband is "Grandpa J," and his mother is "Grandma Wilson."

Picking out a name from the beginning can alleviate confusion. When asked what her grandchildren call her, Deirdre said,

> I was lucky that I made the choice at the birth of my first grandchild to be called "Nana." My husband chose to be called "Papa." My husband's grandmothers and parents were alive, and so were my parents. My former daughter-in-law had two sets of grandparents still alive and both parents. Altogether, there were seven or eight grandmothers. All the grandmothers wanted to be called "Grandma," and I could see trouble ahead with that situation, so I became "Nana," after my own grandmother, who had died. It turned out to be a good choice because everybody calls me "Nana" like it's my name. Even my new daughter-in-law and her children have no trouble calling me "Nana."

Christopher said,

> The awkward issue for kids is what do you call this person? With my stepfather, who is now my children's step-grandfather, I had no interest in calling him "Father" or "Pa," so I settled on "Ed." It became a loving thing, so now the word "Ed" is endearing—like "Mom." It transitioned from formal to a loving thing. I think I called my step-grandmother "Grandma." Kids kind of think of old people as a grandma or a grandpa, so to call them that doesn't seem to create the same emotional concerns. To call your stepfather "Dad" seems like a betrayal. But a grandparent is different because you already start with four grandparents. I called my other step-grandfather "CB," as in Calvin Bicknell. I called one "Nana." The others were "Grandma and Grandpa."

Christopher's stepmother said,

> I think it's true that blood is thicker than water. One Mother's Day, Dick's daughter asked me what she should give me. I said, "I'd like you to call me 'Mom.'" She told everyone at church that I said to call me "Mom." She did for several years, and then she reverted to calling me "Mitzi" like everyone does, and that's just fine. They all call me "Mitzi" now.

Christopher's mother said,

> They call us "Grandpa" and "Grandma." There's really no confusion. If I happen to call when one of the other grandparents have been there or called, then the kids say "Grandma Ann" is calling or "Grandpa

Ed," but usually it's only us who call, and so it's only us who are "Grandpa and Grandma."

Leslie said that she was already called "Grandma" before her family became more complicated, and that's what all the grandchildren call her. She's heard their parents call her "Grandma Leslie" to their children, and she's fine with that. Luckily she doesn't mind, but others who were interviewed had definite likes and dislikes about what they were called.

Because of Stan's profession as a professor in audiology and speech therapy, he was ready with a name for himself when his first grandchild was born—Baba—because it is the first sound many babies say. He said,

> It turned out to be a good decision. Number one, having a name already picked out for myself made it so no one came up with a name I didn't like. Number two, when relationships got complicated later on with divorce and step-grandchildren and such, no one had a problem calling me "Baba." That's my name. It's who I am, and everyone is comfortable with it.

His wife, Dolores, on the other hand, was not as fortunate. She said,

> I always wanted to be called "Grandma," but I hated it when my husband's stepmother was called "Grandma Carter." I thought it was not as personal as I wanted a grandmother to be. I thought that if I was called "Grandma," I could insist that my grandchildren just call me "Grandma" and not add the "Carter," but it didn't turn out that way. There got to be too many grandmothers, and the children resorted to calling me

"Grandma Carter," just like my husband's stepmother. Oh, well.

When I asked several of the people what they call their grandparents or what their grandchildren call them, I got replies with a wide range of terms. I had thought that the most common would be "Grandma and Grandpa" or "Papa and Nana," but not so. People are very creative with what they call grandparents and step-grandparents. Here are a few of their responses:

> My kids call my mom "Mongo" and my dad "Bugga." There's a funny story there.

> We are "Nana and Goppy." "Nana" because it is easy for tiny ones to say. The oldest grandkid couldn't say "grandpa," so we kept "Goppy" because it was cute.

> "Grandma and Grandpa" . . . both sides. But my great-grandparents were "Grandmother and Granddad."

> All we six kids had was my "Gram."

> Reminds me of the Jimmy Stewart movie, *Mr. Hobbs Takes a Vacation*. Hobbs was dubbed by one of the grandsons, "Boom-pa." Now my grandchildren call me "Boom-pa."

> We are "Nana and Bumpa."

> My mom is "Mumsie," my mother-in-law is "Namma," and my other mother-in-law is "Grammie." The grandfathers are "Poppa," "Papa," and "Grampy"!

> We have "Grandpa D," "Grandpa Beard," and "Grandma."

> We are "Nana and Papa."
>
> We're Italian, so my grandmother was "Nonna" and my grandfather was "Nonno."
>
> My grandma in Germany is "Oma."
>
> We have "Grandpa and Grandma" and the great-grandparents are "G-G-pa and G-G-ma."
>
> We have our unique places in our grandchildren's lives. "Papo" and math, "Grammie" and grammar, "Grammie Noodles" and grammar. This is how the children think of us.

When steprelations enter the picture, names and titles can present difficulties. Not everyone agrees on what the protocol should be. Sharon suggests, "Be careful about insisting that they call you 'Grandma' or whatever the other grandkids call you. They may already feel attached to their other grandparents and feel hesitant to address you in the same way. Let them take the lead with how they address you."

On the other hand, Sean says, "The terms 'Grandma' and 'Grandpa' are pretty generic, kind of like what any old person would be called, so I don't think being called 'Grandpa' would be hard for a kid to get used to."

The names may not be important, but having names that the children can use to identify their many different relations *is* important. Children can be more comfortable knowing the distinct places these people have in their lives. A good strategy would be to have a name picked out, as Stan and Deirdre did, before the grandchildren or step-grandchildren come along so confusion can be avoided.

I remember that, as a child, I was always anxious about how to introduce my parents' friends. I knew the friends were called one thing within that circle of friends, usually a first name or a nickname, but I also knew that there was a proper way to make introductions, and I was unsure about the protocol. I thought it involved last names, and I wasn't always sure what those names were. I particularly remember being at a school event and trying to introduce a family friend to my teacher and being uneasy about what to call the friend, since the name we called the friend was more a term of endearment than a name, and I didn't know the friend's last name.

However, I had no problem with my relatives. Each one had a place and a name. I knew I could introduce my relatives properly, and that relieved me as a child. It might seem like a silly thing to be anxious about, but children do tend to become anxious over anything they are unsure about. In blended families especially, anything that can be done to reduce anxiety will be helpful in settling the family into a comfortable routine. Having acceptable names can be a step in that direction.

CHAPTER FOUR

A Step-Grandparent Is Always (and Even More of) a Parent

Caleb had both an advantage and a handicap when he married Charmayne—her parents were both deceased. He didn't have to negotiate that potentially difficult situation of new in-laws, but because they were gone, he didn't have their support, either. Luckily, he still made a resounding success of becoming a grandparent, but it might have been easier if they had been alive. Having the support of the in-laws is important for any marriage to succeed. Of course, it is possible for a new marriage to be successful without the approval of the spouses' parents, but good relationships ease anxiety in the family. When there are already children or other established relationships, it gets complicated to add more, and relations with those parents and grandparents must be established from the beginning.

Tony, for example, has in-laws who don't like him. They make it very clear that they don't like him by visiting with their grandchildren and not speaking to him. They act like he's not there, which makes him feel rejected and stressed. In fact, he said,

> For years they would simply not talk to me for hours after we arrived for a visit at their house in Louisville. They were immediately wrapped up in the grandkids, and my wife's mother often did not even say "hello" to me. Once, I experimented to see how long it would be before she said something to me, but finally had to start a conversation about her gardening after three hours of waiting to see if she would engage me.

Tony's in-laws exhibit petty selfishness that places stress on his marriage and on him because he wants to love his wife's parents and to have their support. It's also stressful for his wife, who feels she has to apologize for their behavior. These grandparents are poor examples for their grandchildren, who see them holding a grudge or being judgmental. Tony summed it up very well when he said, "I believe that to be a great grandparent, you must also remember that you are still a parent as well."

Being a parent does not go away, no matter how old the child grows. I remember my great-grandmother (age 90) moving in with her daughter (age 70) to help, because, as my great-grandmother said, "She's an old woman and needs taking care of."

The parental role does shift somewhat due to circumstances and changing ages. Parents of grown children are presented with all kinds of situations—as many kinds of situations as there are people—some too bizarre to be believed if it didn't happen to them. Parenting grown children through these situations requires a foundational principle of love and a desire to see them develop into adults who can stand on their own, while still giving them the support they need. It's a high wire balancing act that has repercussions for generations.

Sometimes the line between grandparenting and parenting is hard to define. For example, Ellen had to learn where to draw the line on parenting and grandparenting when her daughter got married and had a son, Dillon. She said,

> Having a grandchild puts a different twist on the relationship between my daughter and me. I want to correct all the mistakes I made, and when I see my daughter making the same mistakes, I want to defend my grandchild. I did some things I probably should not have, because I wanted to make Dillon's life smoother than mine had been. I wanted to keep him safe. There was one time when I went into her house and thought that it wasn't clean enough for my grandson. So, I went in and cleaned her house top to bottom and hired someone to clean the air ducts. Then I finally got to the point where I thought that my job is not to make his life perfect. I can't do that. No matter what I do, he has to learn from his own life. I'm trying to make my grandson's life smooth and stress-free and easier. But no matter how much I help, he still has the same parents. I have to remember that I was raised in a really abusive home, but I came out OK. At first I thought my role was to be a substitute parent, but it's not. My job is to have a different kind of relationship with him. I'm his Nana, and that is what I should be.

As Ellen found, a grandparent's role is usually not to be the parent to grandchildren. When parents are present in grandchildren's lives, grandparents have to step back and allow their children and grandchildren to be their own family. However, grandparents can and should be in a supportive position, unless there are extenuating circumstances.

This support sometimes comes even before new marriages are solidified. For example, Deirdre came home from a business trip to find her son's girlfriend and children living in her house. Tom explained,

> I went with my son to help her move after the apartment building she lived in was sold unexpectedly. On such short notice, she didn't have time to find a decent place to live. The apartment she was going to move into smelled of urine and was so dirty that she just stood in the doorway and burst into tears. So, I told her I wouldn't take no for an answer and I moved her into our guest bedroom.

Deirdre said, "I would have done the same thing, but it was still a bit of a shock. They didn't even call me to tell me, so I came home to all these people in my house. However, I'm glad we were able to help. It worked out well. When my son proposed to her, how could she say no after his parents had taken her in?"

Support from a grandmother was also crucial for Shelley's family. When her mother died after the birth of Shelley's youngest sister and Shelley's father did not feel capable of taking care of two little girls,

> Gram came to help and stayed for the next eight or nine years acting as our surrogate mother. She was a strict disciplinarian, but we knew she loved us, and she was there when no one else was. She taught me values and morals, taught me how to work hard, and

instilled in me high standards for whatever I did, including homework or whatever I was assigned to do.

As far as Shelley was concerned, having her grandmother step in was a great blessing. She said, "Grandparents add more to your life. They help smooth over the differences that you have with your parents. They seem to have reached that point in their lives where they can see the bigger picture and help you over the rough spots."

Shelley's grandmother also knew when it was time to leave. When the children were old enough to fend for themselves and when she decided it was time for her son to get married again, she left. It worked, too. He did remarry eventually.

The distinction between supporting and intervening can be difficult to discern. Julie explained,

> Ah, yes. The stubborn teenager. As the oldest [grandchildren] have advanced into the teen years, boy have we been embroiled in conflict. As a grandmother I stand firmly on the side of mom and dad—even when I don't agree with mom and dad. Sometimes your teen is correct. I then take the approach of mother-to-daughter and try to influence the parent over the child.

Notice that Julie did not usurp the parents' role, but supported them in their decision, even though she felt the teen was right. If she supports the parents, they might be more willing to take her advice to lighten up because their position as parents isn't being threatened.

It is important for grandparents to know when to step back from parental responsibilities and when to offer support. Sharon explained,

> Because of the divorce of my parents, I spent a great deal of time with my maternal grandparents. My

mother, older brother, and I lived with them for the first year after the divorce. They were a stabilizing force during that year while my twenty-four-year-old mother tried to make a life for us by returning to college and earning her teaching credentials. My grandmother just loved me and praised me and told me how wonderful I am. She didn't worry about spoiling my cousins, brother, or me. I guess that's because she knew that our parents instilled discipline and set boundaries. She just made us feel like she enjoyed being with us as much as we enjoyed being with her.

Sharon's story brings up another important point—in the face of disaster or divorce that can cause despair and frustration, the grandmother just loved and praised and helped Sharon's family get through that rough time. That was her role.

Caroline had to devise some tactics to handle the new dynamics that came with a new daughter-in-law with different ideas and habits. Caroline had been rather laid back about having everyone clean up after dinner when she invited the family over. She preferred to sit and enjoy her grandchildren for a while and then get everyone to help her for a few minutes before they left. In contrast, her new daughter-in-law wanted everyone to clean up as soon as the meal was finished. Caroline said,

> She insisted everyone, even my son, had to get everything clean before we could do anything else. And she did it on the basis that it wasn't fair for me to cook the dinner and then have a messy house to clean, although I was tired and just wanted to play with the grandchildren after dinner and having to clean meant I had to supervise and help clean, too. So my

son stepped in and helped devise a plan where the cleaning happened quickly, so there was some order and everyone knew what they were supposed to do. That finally satisfied my daughter-in-law, and it was a good plan.

Dealing with ever-changing personalities and situations requires some flexibility. Both Angela and Mitch's daughter and their adopted daughter got divorced. Both times they were drawn into the conflict. Angela said,

> My daughter separated from her husband. After they were separated, he came for Christmas, because I invited him, but he wouldn't stay the whole time, so I sent him home with lots of food. I've invited him for Thanksgiving, too, after the divorce, but he had a girlfriend at the time, so he didn't come. That's when things turned even more negative. He wanted to drag us into the divorce and subpoenaed us to appear in court. We didn't want anything to do with that. We tried to remain impartial. We got a lawyer who made it so we would just have to talk to the judge over the phone. I didn't want the expense or hassle of having to go all that way and get a hotel and meals. Our other daughter's husband actually sat in on the conference call, which was good, because he remembered sequences that I had forgotten. After the separation, I told our ex-son-in-law that we loved him like a son. We still like him. He often came down to talk to us and helped us with my husband, Mitch, after he became ill. When he drops their daughter off at my place, I go out and talk to him and ask him how he is. My daughter and he are better friends now than

when they were married. When he got appendicitis, my daughter took care of him until he was better. Why should I be mad at him? I wasn't married to him. He's a good man, a hard worker, and a good provider. He even still helps my daughter out when she has problems.

Similarly, when their adopted daughter left her husband, Angela and Mitch were dragged into the conflict. Angela said,

> Brenda's husband came over and tried to tell us his side of the story. We knew he hadn't been treating her right and hadn't been good to her for years, but all Mitch said was that he loved Brenda like a daughter and that her husband had better treat her well. We weren't going to get pulled into it. Even so, we were there for Brenda when she decided to leave him, and she came to live with us. We gave her a safe place.

For Angela and Mitch's peace of mind, they tried to stay out of any conflict. It was also important for them to allow both women to be adults and handle their lives on their own and yet know they had someone acting as support in the background.

When conflict rears its ugly head, it is important to have a game plan in mind or a set of personal rules to keep you and the rest of the family in a healthy place. Bethany advises,

> Don't get involved in their marital problems if you can, or do anything that is controlling. I've thought for the last few years, "I will be their good friend and teach if they want to know, but I don't call them to teach or lecture them." I definitely don't want them to think they are under my magnifying glass and

drive them away. My father was always really nice to his nephews and kids, no matter what he thought of them. One nephew who had always been in trouble with all kinds of problems said my father was a kind man, and I learned from that. He sometimes came to my father for help after his own father died. You just be a nice support system. I try to do that with my step-children and step-grandchildren. I'm always there, and I always remember occasions. It takes years, but over time it happened to be a nice outcome that now my husband's kids want me to be there and they talk to me one on one. For instance, I thought his youngest didn't care much for me. She came to visit recently, and I was surprised that she stayed in the kitchen the whole time and talked. I never thought I would be in that position. So you just never give up. Think what will be the best thing for that child, and it will be the best thing for you, too.

That's an interesting point of view—what will be the best for that child will be the best for the grandparent. Good things do seem to come when we put others first. The caution is that the grandparent needs to recognize what really is best for the child. Letting the grandchildren walk all over a grandparent isn't good, either. I recently had a conversation with a friend who told me of her grandmother, who was quite wealthy, and how some of the grandchildren had taken advantage of her, asking for her to pay for houses and condos and cars. It got to the point that the family had to get a lawyer to put the remaining money into a trust and give the grandmother a stipend to live on so the money was not available for the grandchildren to wheedle away. The stipend was large enough for her to feel like she could live as she had, but not large enough to buy houses or cars.

Unfortunately, in this country the statistics are staggering that show how many children and grandchildren defraud older family members out of their money and leave them in poverty. I was made aware of this shameful practice when my sister and I were put in charge of our parents' finances. The staff at the bank let us know how poorly other families had behaved. My sister and I were extra careful to make sure our parents never had to worry about something like that. We accounted for every penny and made sure that all our parents' money went where they wanted it to.

Later, when I volunteered at a retirement center, I was made aware of the same thing happening to some of the residents. One woman was in the retirement center because she had given much of her money to her son to build a mother-in-law apartment onto his house so she could live with him and his wife. When the apartment was finished, the son refused to have her come and even sold the house without reimbursing his mother for all the money she had put into it. She had to enlist the help of another son to help her sue to get her money back, although she did so with a broken heart.

So, no, it is not in the best interests of anyone in a family for anyone to take advantage of anyone else. Lessons in honesty, loyalty, and standing on their own feet are important examples for the whole family so they can learn and recognize ethical behavior. It is still wonderful when family members can help when there is real need, and when problems are seen as opportunities. Many people I interviewed told of times when their families pulled together.

Leslie agrees. She said,

> There are no pitfalls in my family, only joy. Some of the children have problems, but I'm not bothered. I say, "It's not my problem. My job is just to love them unconditionally." My son has a little boy just like he is, and now he has to deal with this little boy who

is always getting into trouble. I don't have to deal with that at all. All I have to do is love them. There is no downside to it because they come to my house, and we interact for a few hours, and then they just go home, and I don't have to worry. My other son's oldest daughter doesn't care how she looks, and I just say you have to love her how she is. With the boy who is always in trouble, you just take him and you love him and give him a good time, and then you send him home.

When asked what happens when the conflict occurs in her house, Leslie said,

I had another grandma, and she was more well-to-do and more proper, and I was always afraid of breaking something or doing something wrong when I was in her house. No matter how good I tried to be, I was afraid of screwing up (and I usually did) and that grandma often disapproved of me. I don't want to be like that. You can always wash off the couch or replace the carpet. The children are what's most important. I will say don't drink grape juice in the living room, but I say it in a way that is kind. I don't want them to worry about doing something wrong.

Leslie's advice is very wise. If children feel any disapproval from an adult, they will become hesitant to be around that disapproving adult.

Sometimes being the grandparent and the parent means helping grandchildren and their parents get along better. Ellen found herself having to counsel her two-year-old grandson about how he treated his mother. She said,

> Dillon went through a phase where when my daughter would pick him up from the babysitter, he would yell, "No! No! I don't want to go with you." That was because he was playing a game or having fun there. My daughter would call me up and cry about it and the fact that she had to work and couldn't just play with him when they went home because things needed to get done and she just can't pay attention to him all the time. He does the same thing at my house because I give him my full attention. Finally, I sat him down and told him he was making his mother cry when he said that, and he needed to make her happy. So when my daughter came to pick up Dillon, he ran over and gave her a big hug and told her he loved her. He really is a darling little guy.

Stan and Dolores have had several times when they stepped in to help their children and grandchildren. Dolores said,

> Maybe that is what *step* really means in family relationships. You step in to help, not only with your steprelations, but with your own children and grandchildren. But then, they are all really yours anyway. We try to help all of them any way we can, if it's within our means. After our children were grown, we had some empty bedrooms. Several times over the years, those bedrooms have been filled for extended periods of time because of job loss, or grandchildren needing a place to stay while they go to college, or when they need to have a place to live while they are in the process of moving. Of course, when our daughter was divorced, she came to live with us until she

could stand on her own again. The only downside is that our storage rooms in the basement have lots of their stuff. I tell them I'm not going to bother cleaning those rooms. They're going to have to clean it all out themselves when we die.

Stan said,

> It's been our privilege to help out financially as well. We've been fortunate to have enough money to help out with house payments from time to time or short-term loans to the children, and we've offered the grandchildren some money to help with tuition for college on occasion as we could. We see that as an investment in our future. The difficulty comes when we can see something going wrong, but we feel it isn't our business to intervene. We are there, though, to pick up the pieces and offer support with a place to stay, a little money, or some advice. We try to be the solid, safe place.

Caroline doesn't have a lot of money or much space. To help her family, she offers her time and what resources she has. She said,

> I offer babysitting. I know what it's like to be a young mother who needs to work, and so when my daughter-in-law decided to go to school to get a degree so she could get a job and help my son, who had some health problems, I offered to babysit. I like to feel useful, and I love playing with the grandchildren. When my step-granddaughter got sick from all the drama going on in her family and with new relations and all, I babysat her, too, and

> even tutored her so she could stay caught up in school. I taught her to knit and crochet, and she really liked that. She got so good at it, I took her to the knitting store and we had lessons on knitting sweaters. She still knits amazing sweaters. I think it calms her down.

Roslyn and Stephen have blurred the lines between grandparent and parent as they've raised their grandchildren. Roslyn said, "They are our children, and we feel like they are our children."

Stephen said, "One word of advice. If anything happens to your grandchildren, be sure to make yourself available. Don't say it's not your problem. It is. I always say, 'Small children, small worries. Big children, big worries.' But you have to be there for them."

Stephen makes an important point. He said to make yourself available and to be there for them. He did not say to interfere. Sometimes that is a fine line. In my family, I offer things I can do, and if that is in line with what is needed, the family takes me up on it. There are times when they ask when I haven't offered, which is all right, but it is usually something I've already offered previously. The benefit for me is that I often get to spend some time with my grandchildren.

Diane said,

> You have a different relationship with grandchildren when you spend time alone with them. We have a closer relationship with Riley than the others whose families are intact. My husband Stephen is a fun, loving grandpa, and Riley loves him and loves to be with him. His half-sister, little Emma, really became attached to Stephen. Riley understood that his half-sister wasn't related, but Emma didn't. We had her come to family parties, and she just joined

right in. Now they have moved to another state to be near their mother's parents, so we don't know how we will maintain that relationship, but we intend to stay close.

Staying close is what family is all about. The significance of the efforts the grandparents in this chapter have made to be present in their grandchildren's lives is that they've made a difference when it was needed. The outcomes to their stories could have been much different if they hadn't offered to help. Yet, they also understand boundaries and try not to interfere.

Chapter Five

An Island of Peace

The No-Judgment Buffer Zone

We smile when someone says that they love being a grandparent because they can hand the kids back to the parents at the end of a visit. We smile because it's true—unless they're living with us. There are times when grandparents or step-grandparents must assume a caretaker role, but most of the time we get to enjoy the bustle and noise of visits and then the blessed peace and quiet when everyone's back in their appropriate homes. We can stand at the door, waving good-bye with big smiles on our faces and watch our children with their children as they drive away. Then we can shut the door. As Leslie said, "There is no downside to it because they just go home, and I don't have to worry."

Because we don't have the responsibility of being the primary caregiver, grandparents can be the non-judgmental buffer zone for our families that can make us a safe place or, as Sharon said, "A soft place to land."

Being the grandparent offers opportunities to help grandchildren have experiences in a safe setting that can help them grow in ways that parents might not think of or be capable of providing. For example, Ellen found that she could provide an opportunity for her grandson, Dillon, that also helped her daughter see a new way to interact with him. She said,

> Dillon often comes to my house, and I have him help me with the cooking. My daughter and her husband see him all the time, and they think of him as a baby, so when she cooks, she wants him out of the room. One time I was baking cookies, and I put him on the kitchen counter and showed him how to roll the cookies in sugar, and he loved it. I would make a ball of cookie dough and hand it to Dillon, and he rolled it in the sugar and put it on the cookie sheet. My daughter came in right then and was amazed. She acted like she never thought of that, but now she tries to have him help. He has a stool at my house, and when he sees that I'm about to cook, he says, "I will help you, Nana." I was able to introduce new things for him, both in experience and food. The other day he helped me make a salad for his grandpa. Dillon loves olives, so it was covered with black olives.

In a gentle way, Ellen helped her daughter see opportunities to interact with Dillon and to give Dillon the confidence that comes with doing some things himself—under her supervision, of course.

I had a similar experience when my oldest grandson was learning to drive. After he got his permit, I let him do the driving in my car whenever we went somewhere. I had to chuckle when he said, "You're easy to drive with because you don't yell." I told him I'd taught all of my own children how to drive and was over the yelling part. I think that sometimes the grandparents, because they've already gone through so much, can be more relaxed in situations that would normally make parents upset.

As step-grandparents and grandparents, we can provide the space and emotional stability that children need. Sharon told of how, after her parents' divorce, she and her brother and mother lived in a two-bedroom apartment in a poorer part of town. She loved going to her grandparents' home: "They had a big house with twelve acres on the outskirts of town, and it was like our own park with a swing set, a pond, basketball hoop, and many places to roam and explore. I loved going there where I could experience space and peace. The best part was just being with them and being included in their day-to-day activities." When Sharon's world was in turmoil, the space and peace and attention she got from her grandparents were important in her life. Other grandparents and grandchildren told of similar experiences.

Mitzi, Christopher's stepmother, said,

> We had a peaceful place. We had a happy place. When we first got married, I don't think Dick, Christopher's father, knew how to interact with his own children. Their home was very proper. Our home is exactly the opposite, and we just had fun. I think they liked the peace, and eventually their dad knew how to act with them better. I could tell being in our home was relaxing for them. When we moved to a new house, they had their own rooms, but they often chose to stay together of their own free will because they thought it was fun. I don't think it would have

turned out as well if we'd said, "You have to stay two to a room, and this is who you will have as a roommate." We also let them stay in their own schools so they could be with their own friends and went to a lot of parent-teacher conferences driving back and forth from school to school.

Mitzi and Dick achieved the peaceful, happy atmosphere in their home because of the plan of action that they agreed upon. Mitzi explained,

> My husband said we have to have a neutral home, and we'll agree with each other. He said "I'll support you in what you say, and you support me, and we won't let anyone divide us." That was the success of Dick's and my marriage. We told the children that if you live here, you live here happy. You have another home to go to if you don't like it here. We said we didn't have happiness before, and we want it now, so our home is going to be a happy home, and that is what it is for our children and our grandchildren.

Step-grandparents sometimes have the disadvantage of coming into the picture later than the natural grandparents, but they can be an influence on the lives of their new family members if they're willing to work at it. The important principle to remember is that time and effort are required, as well as establishing a non-judgmental relationship from the start.

Leslie said that being non-judgmental has made a huge difference in her family. For example, she said that the other day, her grandson kept bugging his mother about something, and his mother said, "Go ask Grandma." The grandson said, "Grandma always says yes." That made Leslie laugh. She said it typified her relationship with her grandson—a relationship she has cultivated over several years with all the grandchildren, step and natural. She explained,

> I'm physically demonstrative with them. When the thirteen-year-old sees me she always gives me a hug, as well as the seven-year-old boy who thinks he is too old for a hug. I tell him to come over and hug me, and he eventually does. There is something about the touch. I believe that love comes through your touch. You don't hug people you don't like. You convey gentleness through touch on the arm or shoulder or a whole hug. It's something that keeps you connected. It's not like shaking hands with someone. That can be cold. However, you can't start when they're a teenager. You have to start when they're little and not embarrassed by it. I started it with my own children when they were small. When my son had to go overseas for several months, I hugged him when he came home. He hugged me back, and he said that what he missed most while he was gone was his mother's touch.

Leslie, Ellen, Julie, and others mentioned the importance of touch. My own grandchildren know they have to hug me when they come and when they leave. It was a little awkward getting the step-grandchildren to do the same, but after the initial strangeness of building new relationships, it's more natural now. Treating all the grandchildren the same is important in smoothing over the divide between the grandchildren who have been there since birth and those who have come in later. It is vital, however, that interactions should be natural and not mandated.

Tom's experience with his grandparents affects the way he interacts with his grandchildren and step-grandchildren. He said,

The rules for grandkids shouldn't be mandates or restrictive like my paternal grandmother's. They should be things like no whining, no fighting amongst themselves, common courtesy, and such. If you have more rules and more restrictive rules than that, you become another set of parents, and you'll lose that healthy one-off relationship that makes grandparenting so enjoyable for both the grandparents and the grandkids.

Deirdre agrees. She said,

Tom and I recently had two of the grandchildren come stay with us while my son took his new wife away for a vacation for her birthday. I decided that I wasn't going to have much in the way of rules while the kids were here, and pretty much all I made them do was clean up their messes and go to bed on time and brush their teeth. The rest I let slide, like taking baths or combing hair or even eating all their meals. They're of the age when they can pretty much entertain themselves, but to keep them out of trouble, I had some little craft things to make, some games they could play, some videos they could watch, and other activities where we could just play together. It turned out that with no friction and no real demands, they were eager to help vacuum and help out in other ways. We even made a birthday cake and a birthday dinner for their stepmother for when she and my son returned. It turned out pretty well and was a peaceful visit. I want my grandchildren to look at our house as a pleasant, peaceful place to be, like an oasis. When my son and his wife came to pick up the children, they were surprised that there hadn't been any conflict.

When possible, lack of conflict can be a blessing. Deirdre also said, "I do have one rule and that is for everyone to leave their baggage home when they come to my house. They can all behave nicely for the few hours they are here. At this stage in our lives, I don't feel like we need to hash over problems when the family gets together. They can talk to each other on their own time if they have problems."

Children who have experienced abandonment are often especially hungry for the attention an adult can give. For example, Christopher, who has step-grandparents and stepparents, said, "You have to realize you're going to invest some time in this. You're going to practice being a stepparent or step-grandparent. It can't start from the child. They want to trust and are ready to love. Their instinct is to be loved, but they're going to wait to see if they have to protect themselves or what. Build a relationship of trust."

Grandparents don't have to provide the same opportunities as other grandparents to be worthwhile or valued in their families' lives. Christopher also said, "My children benefit differently from each set of grandparents. The common denominator is that if grandparents invest in a child's life by being there and paying attention to him or her, there are tremendous dividends in that the child will watch and listen to the grandparent."

Those dividends can be seen in teaching moments and strengthened relationships. As Gene said, his grandfather was able to teach him in "a grandfatherly sort of way."

Lily, whose family has several layers of steps (step-grandparents, stepparents, step-siblings, and half-siblings) relied heavily on her grandparents and step-grandfather as a child when her father abandoned the family. She said, "My step-grandpa saved us when my parents got divorced. He gave us rides and did the gardening and gave me rides to parties, even if he picked me up at midnight. My other grandpa was still there. He always helped me with my homework. He remembers things he read and gave me a love of books." The time and effort shown by Lily's grandfathers played a huge part in making her life a success.

Bethany has found that circumstances change with each child as they get older. However, she says that the way she treats each one is always consistent, so they know they can come to her with their problems. She said,

> I think that once they get to a certain age, maybe it's different for each child, but they become your friends. I learned to only give them advice when they asked, but for the most part you treat them with support, and be happy, and step out of the position you had when you told them what to do. So you just be upbeat and supportive. They don't want to disappoint you, no matter what age they are.

Notice that by being upbeat and supportive, Bethany has made herself the kind of person that her family does not want to disappoint. Wanting the approval of a grandparent can be a stronger motivating factor than getting gifts or other more tangible things that grandchildren might get from grandparents.

Shelley, whose mother died after the birth of the Shelley's youngest sister, remembers her grandmother as someone who loved unconditionally, "Gram was always supportive. I remember when she took the time to do some hand-sewing on a dress I was making in a hurry for a concert. I was touched that she took the time to do so. And it turned out to be a really pretty dress. Sky-blue polyester (ugh)." Shelley also said,

> She always loved us. She demonstrated it and told us so. She also told us she loved us by demanding that we do better than average people. She'd say, 'It may be good enough for them, but not for you.' That gave us pretty high standards to reach for, but we also knew she loved us, and we didn't want to disappoint her.

In troubled times, sometimes, grandparents or step-grandparents can provide a haven from family storms. Stan said,

> I was building a cabin in the mountains when my grandsons were teenagers and their family was going through difficulties. I often took them with me to help me build because I really needed the help and they needed to get out of a bad situation. I learned all about Pink Floyd and Depeche Mode, and they learned about Dutch oven cooking, how to pound a nail, and how to wire electrical fixtures. We never actually talked about their problems when they were teenagers, but later on (now they are in their twenties and thirties), they often come to me for advice.

"It's interesting how establishing a non-judgmental relationship plays out in different situations," said Deirdre.

> Recently, our grandson and his father had a huge fight, and he stormed off to live with his mother. He wouldn't even speak to his father for weeks, and when his brother told him he was being stupid, he wouldn't talk to any of his siblings, either. We had him come for the weekend a couple of times and just hung out with him. Didn't say a word about the argument with his father. One night we were watching a show where a mother and daughter got in a huge

fight, and all kinds of terrible things happened until they finally made up. Under his breath, I heard him say, "I ought to think about that." The next week was his stepsister's birthday, and we were surprised to see him at the party, helping with the food and setting up chairs, and even more surprised to see him hug his father when he left. Not long after that he was back living with his father.

There was a time when Angela and Mitch's adopted daughter's son was not doing well. Angela said,

> Josh started drinking and missing school and just being wild. We couldn't do much except tell him we love him. Josh came to us when Mitch got really sick and said he could help us and we could help him if he moved in with us. He would help with Mitch and help me put Mitch to bed at night. Mitch was a big guy, and it was hard for me to move him. Once we got Mitch in bed, Josh would say to me, "You can go now." He and Mitch would talk for a long time each evening. Mitch would tell him to get his life together and stop drinking and go to church and go to college. Josh did clean up his act some. He drinks less now, and he is going to college. When Mitch died, Josh had a terrible time. That summer was hard on him. Josh came over recently to help me clean out a room. He said it was like coming home. Another time I asked him to go buy some mulch for the garden, and I gave him the money and some for helping me. He said I didn't need to pay him, because this is his home, too.

Home—a place of refuge and a place to come back to. It is significant that being non-judgmental and just loving Josh made him feel that he could come to Angela and Mitch, not only to get help himself, but also to offer help when help was needed.

The need for a home was expressed by several people. For example, Melanie's need for grandparents and their home was extreme. She said,

> My dad was an alcoholic. My mom and dad fought a lot—the breaking-of-lamps and Mom's-head-being-held-down-under-water kind of fighting. My grandmother and the farm were our refuge. Time with my Gram was simple and loving and quiet and, most of all, predictable! I continue to talk to my Gram daily. I think of her as my guardian angel and ask for her help and guidance still. I know she is there for me, as always.

Not all grandparent-grandchild relationships are positive, but they can have a profound effect just the same. Myfanwy remembered,

> Going over to my grandparents' house, there was kind of an expectation that I knew I was going to get criticized. At that age I didn't understand that it was out of love. I didn't understand that my Grandma liked me. I think I was a pretty sensitive kid. I know now she was trying to help me be better. It teaches me something about how to interact with kids who don't understand adult emotions.

Caroline remembered one instance where things did not go well. It was a time when she wishes she had behaved differently. "I could have handled it better," she said. Her teenage grandson was causing huge problems in the family, and her son had just about had it with the boy. At a family get-together at Caroline's house, her son ranted about all the bad things his son had done. "My grandson hadn't come to the party, so I only heard my son's side of it," Caroline said.

> I got angry, too, and of course I took my son's side. When my daughter-in-law said she had to go pick up that boy from work, I told her that if she left my house to be with him, she didn't need to come back. She just looked at me like I was being silly and went to get her son. A while later, she walked back into my house with my grandson and proceeded to smooth things over between her husband and her son. The party turned out all right and ended peacefully. My daughter-in-law never said anything to me about what I'd said to her. She just ignored it like it hadn't been worth dealing with, which made me even madder for a while until I simmered down. It turned out that I didn't know the whole story and had jumped the gun. It was best forgotten. I learned my lesson, though. I've never let anything like that happen again.

The lesson to be learned from Caroline's story is that taking sides can be dangerous. This situation could have resulted in a rift that would have been difficult to get over. As it was, the action of the daughter-in-law saved the situation.

Roslyn and Stephen have been there for their grandchildren in stressful times, and their grandchildren know they can come to their grandparents for help. Roslyn said,

> Our Charlotte called crying because her father called her saying he is dying. He never calls for anything, not even for holidays, not Christmas, not anything. He never calls unless he wants something. Any time

he calls, Charlotte ends up crying for days. Her father had a stroke and needed someone to come and take care of him, so he wanted Charlotte to drop out of college and come take care of him. He lives in Maui and it is so expensive, but he didn't offer any money for her living expenses. She asked us for help. We talked to the nurses, and they are trying to find insurance for him or Medicaid or something. He never paid child support or taxes, so he's in real trouble. That's the kind of guy he has become. I don't like him. I am afraid of him breaking out in one of his rages. We try to be civil to him, but we couldn't offer any money to him to have whatever needs to be done. However, we did tell Charlotte to stay in school and something would be done for her father.

Situations can become more complicated when dealing with all the extended relations. The significance of the way Roslyn and Stephen handled this situation is that they did what they could to smooth over the problem by simply offering comfort and setting in motion a possible solution. And they were able to comfort their granddaughter, who was reassured because her grandparents stepped in to do what they could.

In most cases, it doesn't take a lot of money or grandiose gestures to make things better. Ashley said of her parents, Diane and Randy,

> They spend more time with Riley and Emma rather than pay for things. Sleepovers are what Riley really enjoyed. They also do fun activities like the park. They make more of an investment of time, even before my brother died. Because of my parents' example, we all made an effort to be in Riley's life, so he has aunts

and uncles and cousins who are a big part of his life. My parents tried to be there at least once a week and extended that to Emma.

Diane added,

> It tickles me that Emma calls me "Grandma." My husband and I talked about it a long time before we ever took the step, because we knew that if we had her coming with Riley, it would be a commitment and go on for a long time. I just figured that when she got older her parents would explain the relationship, and we could still be friends. It would kind of be like finding out that Santa Claus isn't real. My other kids were good sports about it. Ashley was the most, but my other girls would get gifts for her, too. They were always good natured about that as well, and they were sweet with her, but they didn't have any kind of relationship beyond that. I think it's good that we can give Riley and Emma a solid foundation of family when none of their other grandparents lived anywhere near.

Diane and Randy are also good examples for their own children of how to treat others.

Caleb grew up in a family where he became estranged from his parents, but found a refuge in his grandparents. He wants to provide that same refuge for his step-grandchildren.

> When you're in a blended family, you have to be willing to sacrifice. I feel that grandchildren should not be affected, that it should be a blessing in their life to have grandparents. I am closer to my grandparents than I was ever to my parents. I grew up next

to them, and they taught me everything that I know. I've been estranged from my parents and brothers and sisters, but I do see my cousins. My grandparents gave me unconditional love. It was my grandparents who I went to when I needed wisdom and financial help. It's my grandparents who taught me that love is sacrifice.

Love is sacrifice. The grandparents interviewed for this book exemplify sacrifice. They have spent time and effort, have given financial help when possible, and, most importantly, have withheld judgment in order to benefit their families.

CHAPTER SIX

Interacting with All the Exes Who May or May Not Live in Texas

Relationships are not always smooth or comfortable. With shifting families come shifting circumstances, and sometimes it's hard to know how to treat family or ex-family members when marital ties have been broken or feelings have been hurt. It takes courage and compassion to maintain the types of relationships that make life, for the children and you and everyone else in the family, the best that it can be.

For example, after years of family drama, all of Lily's family, including her stepfamily, are friends. She feels that being friends is important in maintaining relationships that benefit her and her children. In fact, they're such good friends that her grandfather and her step-grandfather and grandmother actually lived in the same house for a while. She also feels comfortable enough with her extended family that "we often stay with them." This friendship makes interacting with the members of her family more comfortable for her and her children and makes her family's life richer.

Caleb also believes in maintaining good feelings among the various steps and in-laws in his family, for the sake of the children. He said, "We have been very, very careful about how we include the biological father and never ever say negative things about him, or to each other, because we want them to be part of the family. The kids need that, and we want them to have it." However, Caleb also made it a point to explain that maintaining such relationships is not always easy, especially when there have been hurt feelings or other baggage that can cause estrangement. He said, "When you're in a blended family, you have to be willing to sacrifice. I feel that grandchildren should not be affected, that it should be a blessing in their lives to have grandparents."

What Lily and Caleb feel about stepfamilies is supported by comments by several others that I interviewed. The consensus is that guardian parents' attitudes toward former spouses dictate the children's relationships with the former spouse's family—these guardian parents are the gatekeepers who allow or prevent interaction between family members. In families where there is animosity between the parents after divorce, children often lose contact with grandparents, aunts and uncles, and cousins on the side of the parent they do not live with. Another consequence of conflict between parents is that the children suffer and become distressed as they try to juggle their feelings and relationships. On the other hand, parents who are civil or even friendly with exes allow their children to maintain family relationships and enjoy family events.

For example, Mitzi said,

> There is no problem at all getting the families together. Whenever we had an occasion or dinner or something, we always told them what it was and

> what time it would be, and then we tried to let them do their thing. Then when they came to our house, they were there because they wanted to be. We never talked about the other spouse to the children, because that was their parent. It was important to recognize that they still had parents they loved. When we were first married, Elizabeth moved in with me, and Ann wasn't happy with that. Ed is a peacemaker, and he helped Ann become OK with that. It's not that we didn't have problems. It's just that we were able to work through them.

A hugely important principle involves forgiveness and acting with restraint—an aspect that is one of the sacrifices that Caleb mentioned as being necessary in blended families.

One example is what happened in Stan and Dolores's family. Their former son-in-law hijacked the children and took them to another state. He was a lawyer and pulled strings to get custody of the children. It took years before Stan and Dolores and their daughter, the children's mother, were able to negotiate visits with the grandchildren. To their great sorrow, when the children finally came for a visit, much of the relationship between them and the children had eroded. Stan said,

> It was obvious that their father had been feeding them a bunch of lies about us from things the kids said, but we were careful to never say anything bad about their father. We just tried to help the kids have a good time while they were with us. Eventually the kids could see for themselves that their father had lied to them. The oldest boy even confronted him about it. When they were older, most of them came to visit us on their own or demanded that their dad let them come see us

a couple of times a year. It could have turned out so much worse if we'd retaliated against their father.

In fact, the irony in this situation is that the negative things said by the children's father actually came back to bite him. If Stan and Dolores had retaliated, then the children might have felt that their father was justified in what he had told them.

Another good example is what happened in Deirdre's family. "When my daughter-in-law left my son, I was devastated," said Deirdre.

> She wasn't just my daughter-in-law. She'd been my daughter's best friend before she married my son, and I'd known her since she was fifteen. She'd been in our house often as a teenager. I'd even gone to her high school graduation when her family didn't care to go and had given her a bouquet of flowers to make it special. Over the years, we did things together, and we had a good relationship. When the divorce turned bitter and she flipped out with all kinds of extreme self-destructive behavior, I became concerned for my grandchildren. I could have condemned her and tried to turn the children against her, but that wasn't right. I knew we had to maintain a friendly relationship with her, not only to make it easier for the children, but so we didn't lose them ourselves, and so we could monitor what was happening with the children. I knew that we couldn't have an influence on them, or her, if they weren't close to us.

Deirdre said that her son was upset that she, as his mother, still tried to maintain a relationship with his ex-wife. He thought that anyone in the family who did so was being disloyal to him. Deirdre finally explained to him, "I want access to my grandchildren, and I also want to know what is going on. If I go to pick the children up from her house or if we see her at a school event, I don't want the children to be uncomfortable, and I want to discuss the children with her, which we do. My continued relationship with her is a safety net for the family."

Leslie makes it a point to bond with her daughters-in-law. She includes them in the girls' nights that she organizes every once in a while, so it's not just her and the granddaughters, but the daughters-in-law, too—even her ex-daughter-in-law. She said, "I feel it's important for my relationship with the grandchildren to have good relationships with their mothers." Because she has maintained good relationships all around, she knows what is happening in her family and can help where needed. It also takes the conflict out of her own life.

Sharon and her family have also experienced difficulties in sorting out relationships. She said,

> Well, both my parents have remarried, so my children have two step-grandparents. It can be a challenge because my parents are civil with one another, but not friendly, so it has made many family events stressful. I constantly have to decide which pair to invite to birthday parties, graduation celebrations, holidays, etc. It makes me feel put in the middle, and I think, to an extent, it does the same to my children. They are hesitant to talk to one set of grandparents about the fun they had with another set.

The strained relationships affect the children, but they also affect Sharon as she tries to juggle invitations and events. That kind of strain puts stress on her and the whole family—a stress that isn't necessary, but that can create anxiety for everyone.

Interacting with exes requires restraint and tact, but it can be worthwhile in the long run. Tom said,

> I find being with my son's ex-in-laws extremely stressful, but I try to treat them kindly for the sake of my grandchildren. The other night, I went to a concert where my grandchildren and step-grandchildren were performing, so there were several layers of ex- and stepparents and grandparents there. Afterwards, everyone wanted pictures, so I ended up taking pictures with all their different cameras. My son's ex-mother-in-law is pretty clueless about personal space, and she kept crowding up against my arm to see the pictures I'd just taken. I had to work at keeping a friendly smile on my face. The last thing I wanted was to have the children be uncomfortable, or for them to recognize that there was tension there. It was their night to shine.

Tom's unselfishness while he was in an uncomfortable situation brought peace to those attending the event and also allowed the focus to remain on the children. It truly is selfish to insist that your own hurt feelings are most important and to demand that the attention be on you rather than on the children.

One of the truly unselfish practices I found as I interviewed people was the way they treated all the children in families and ex-families the same. Ellen explained the principle of unselfishness when she said,

> I was raised in a blended family, so maybe I'm more aware of how hurtful it is to see how the other grandparents treat step-siblings. So I hope I don't replicate those feelings. They notice. The sad fact of the matter is that children pick up on feelings and emotions,

> regardless of actions. There are some things you can't help. For example, my husband has other grandchildren from a previous marriage. I am very close to some of his granddaughters, but I don't have the same relationship with them that I do with my own grandson. I love them, I really do, but the relationship is not the same. I try very hard to treat them all equally, as far as you can from a distance. If I send one something, I send the others something. I focus the same amount of time. No matter your feelings, your actions are what are important.

The old adage of *actions speaking louder than words* really proves true in such instances.

One action that can be controlled is the way we speak about others in the family. Roslyn and Stephen had their grandchildren living with them and had to watch what they said about their children's parents. Roslyn said,

> The girls' father never paid a penny of child support. It's the same with Tim's mother, who we've always tried to treat well. In the meantime, Tim's mother is still in Georgia, and she has come out here once. She says she loves and thinks about us and says we're the greatest people. We try not to talk bad about the other spouses and try to make the best about it.

The result is that their grandchildren's parents feel comfortable interacting with Roslyn and Stephen, which makes things easier for everyone.

However, being a peacemaker doesn't mean that you should stop protecting the children. Even though she was trying to smooth over relationships in her family, Roslyn was put in the position of having to stand up for her granddaughters' rights. She said, "The father of the girls is very controlling. He is the biggest control freak I have ever met. He was so terrible to Charlotte I even called him a name once, which I never do. He believes that a woman has no right to even open her mouth. The girls don't want to have anything to do with him."

Stephen added, "Their relationship with their father was heartbreaking. It was a relief for them to come to us and not listen to complaints and fights and having one parent explain one thing to them and the other something else." So sometimes grandparents have to act in the role of protector and provider of refuge, no matter how much they may want to avoid conflict.

Maintaining relationships is important, but it should be done with wisdom. For example, Melinda and her husband had to know where to draw the line with their relationship with her husband's ex-in-laws, especially because those relationships are complicated. Melinda married a man who had a son. His ex-wife had decided she didn't want the responsibility of motherhood and had moved across country, so she didn't have anything to do with her ex-husband or son. Melinda said,

> When we started dating a year after his wife left, *her* parents were still having weekend visits with their grandson and having my husband and his son over a couple Sundays a month for dinner. They welcomed me to those dinners and were *so* warm and loving to me. As my husband and I got more serious and marriage was anticipated, they were happy for us and for their grandchild to have a mom.

However, even with such good relationships established at the beginning, problems came up. Melinda said,

> They did overcompensate for their daughter leaving by giving their grandson anything he wanted on his

visits and taking him to movies that were questionable for his age. The problems came later when we had more children who were then their step-grandchildren. They have always treated them like their own, and that is wonderful in a lot of ways, but these kids have a different mom (me!) who does *not* approve of some of the overcompensation and special treatment that happens. So, there's a division. As the kids have grown, it has become harder to kindly refuse the cell phone for the ten-year-old and the *Lord of the Rings* marathon for the six-year-old. There's a bit of resentment on both sides because we have different ideas of raising children, and now that there's a present mom, me, they don't as easily get to break the rules.

What has helped Melinda and her husband is that they discussed what they want for their children with each other and are on the same page. She said,

Our goal is to raise selfless and responsible children, and we don't see excess as the way to teach that. However, the pile of Christmas presents still grows every year, and we have stopped trying to compete there. I'm sad to say that the best thing we did for this situation was to move states away. They now call and write and send gifts and visit for special occasions, but they are not in our daily life, and it's easier to raise the children with the values we want for them. We love the step-grandparents! We just can't live with them. They are welcome at our home any time, and we visit theirs once a year.

Sometimes relationships with extended ex-relations can be harmful in other ways. Christopher's stepfather's ex-wife was abusive to her own children, and that affected how those children acted toward Christopher and his natural siblings. He said, "Blending that family was impossible. We hated each other. They were mean, and we were not mean. They were sarcastic, and we were not. When my grandfather came to stay, my stepbrother was really rude to him. I don't think they even had a relationship with their own grandmother." Christopher said that it was important to "set some ground rules for the relationship and then coach if people are not doing that correctly. My stepfather would get after his stepchildren, and then the next moment they would be in his arms for a hug. They knew he loved them." Ground rules allow children and adults alike to know how to behave. Ground rules can also help turn uncomfortable situations into more comfortable situations because a standard operating procedure has been set.

In interacting with exes, personal feelings sometimes have to be ignored for the sake of the children and grandchildren—and also peace in your own marriage. Bethany said of her husband's ex-wife, "When I'm with the grandchildren by myself, we have a good time, but when she's there, the dynamics change. She's totally possessive and insecure, especially when I am around the kids that she felt were hers already. In her mind, they're her children and grandchildren."

Bethany recalled one very uncomfortable family gathering:

> For example, my husband's ex-wife was very upset that we were there for one Christmas morning, and she was angry that the kids were playing with my husband, her ex-husband. She thought he was intruding because he hadn't been there when they were young. I just stayed in the background and didn't take the initiative to go over and play with the kids. It didn't affect me because I have plenty of time with them without her there. I don't want

to make the kids uncomfortable, and I'm not going to have my feelings hurt when they run up to her and love her. I'm not going to be too sensitive about it.

Bethany exhibits unselfishness by putting the children's feelings first and also by acknowledging that, at certain times and places, it is just better to step back. She knows that, at other times and places, she can be more demonstrative.

Caroline has social anxiety, so dealing with exes and steps and in-laws is very stressful for her. She said,

> I don't like meeting new people. It makes me very uncomfortable, but I want my children and grandchildren to visit me, even if they bring all these strange people into my home that I'm not familiar with. I've learned to ask lots of questions and smile a lot. If people are answering questions about themselves and telling about this or that, I don't have to talk much. If I find out that one of them can play the piano or the guitar or sing, I ask them to perform for me, and I give them lots of praise. I also don't have to talk if they are performing. It takes the pressure off me, and it makes them feel good.

Caroline has found that focusing on others takes the pressure off of her and also creates good feelings all around. She added, "A few times, it's made it so these strangers become my friends as much as they are my grandchildren's friends, which is a good thing. It makes my life better, too."

Angela also makes the effort to retain good feelings with her daughters' exes. She said, "I keep a friendly relationship with my daughter's ex-husband, so he feels comfortable dropping his daughter off at my house or picking her up. I ask him how he's doing, and we talk for a while when he comes. He doesn't usually come in. I go out to his car and talk to him there."

Angela also tries to maintain good relationships with her adopted daughter's ex-husband. She said,

> I often drove the kids up to their dad's house when it was time for them to have weekends with him. I talked to him and asked him how he was. I tried to be pleasant with him. If he came to one of the kids' games or school events, I would tell him how good he was to come. Later, he married the woman he should have married in the first place, and he became a better father because of her. She often would come over and talk to me at these things, and we would sit and have a nice conversation. I think she made him go to them. Even his son, Josh, says he finally married who he should have.

Mitzi echoed this sentiment when she said, "One of Dick's sons said his parents both married someone they wanted and they're better off, and that's how I see it. There are situations where some people just aren't good together. So we feel lucky to have each other now, and our good relationships benefit the whole family."

Roslyn and Stephen try to treat their ex-son-in-law with respect with the result that, as Roslyn said, "He most of the time respects us, too, although I am afraid of him sometimes. When he was sick, Charlotte asked us to send someone from the church to talk with him, because we've raised her with the church like her mother wanted. He said definitely not. He didn't want anyone from our church. I just told him we would pray for him. He couldn't say much about that." Roslyn and Stephen were put in the position of wanting to ease their granddaughter's fears about her father, and they handled it gracefully by only offering help and not pushing. It was important that their granddaughter could go to them for help, but not that they involve themselves to the point that they interfered where they weren't wanted.

Diane and Randy have also tried to be friendly with their ex-daughter-in-law, Bridget. Diane said,

> We just had a really good relationship. It took time for that relationship to evolve because it was really weird at first. But now, her new husband, Greg, is really friendly with us, too. Bridget and Greg always sat with us at the children's games. When we went to pick up Riley and Emma, Greg would come to the door and visit. It's more pleasant if you're all nice to each other. I think that we will be involved with these people for years, for the rest of our lives, actually. So I would tell Bridget that we're all related through Riley. Because our son died, it made things special. It was our son's second wife who was jealous of our relationship with Bridget and Greg. When Bridget's mother was in town, she came to the door and gave us a big hug. See, it's better if you're pleasant.

Being involved with these people for the rest of our lives means that we, as grandparents and parents, need to establish the types of relationships we want to maintain for a very long time. Sometimes doing so requires effort on our part to understand the family culture of the others we have to deal with and to figure out how to deal with them. As Ellen said,

> There is such a difference dealing with the steps because they are so different from us. My step-granddaughter is the oldest of my grandchildren, and my daughter-in-law is very young. She had the baby when she was only eighteen. The step-granddaughter

was raised by her own grandparents, who are really in the parenting role. That grandmother was really worried because she thought my son would love his son more than the little girl. Now I am having similar feelings. It is hard when I have a new grandson, and here is a little girl I need to have a relationship with who is spoiled, although she can be sweet and precocious. Still, there are so many things about her that are against everything I am for, such as she is still using a pacifier. I can't step in and criticize. The other hard part is that, of course, her grandparents prefer her to my grandson. I don't want that. I really, really work hard not to treat them differently. The fact is that I feel differently toward them. That doesn't mean I don't love her and cuddle her and send her presents, but she reacts differently to me, too. Already I see that my little granddaughter will grow up closer to her other grandparents, and that's a sorrow to me. All I can do is let her know I love her, too. Being impartial is hard.

Being impartial can be hard. But the fact that Ellen and others even have viable relationships with exes and steps is significant because their relationships will have effects that will last for generations.

CHAPTER SEVEN

Holidays, Traditions, Events—Oh, My!

The things that are most memorable for a family are often events complete with traditions, activities, and food. Events create a situation where people can interact with each other, share news with each other, and eat. Events mean someone has gone to the trouble of planning the event, getting there, taking time out of schedules to be somewhere, and preparing food. Family traditions from one family can be incorporated into the blended family. Then everyone can be enriched. My favorite memories are of family events where many people came and good food was served.

For children, events have huge significance. Children are typically participators rather than organizers. They are usually not the ones who plan events, but those events are important to them—especially if the children are performing in some capacity or being included as part of the group, or even if the event is just part of a tradition. Events are even more important if family members show up to support the children and to show approval of their efforts. When the family gets together and the children are included, it signifies belonging, continuity, and worthiness to belong.

Now that she has grandchildren, Ellen has discovered the joy of including them in her holiday traditions. She said, "My daughter and I always got together to put up the Christmas tree, and I'm kind of picky. I have ornaments that I've collected from all over the world, and I wanted them placed just so on the tree." However, her perfectionism lessened when her grandson came into the picture. She said,

> You find that, when you have a two-year-old helping, you don't care so much about how the tree looks. The bottom half of my tree is far more heavily decorated than the top, but he was having so much fun doing it that I had fun just watching him. He would stand back and look at the tree that he had decorated and feel proud of what he'd done. It helped emphasize the magic of Christmas and families. I know that sounds cheesy, but there really is a magic there.

Ellen found another way of including Dillon in her cherished traditions. She said, "I collect Grinch paraphernalia, and I have a little Who village with the little Who characters and the Grinch lair that I put out at Christmas. Dillon loves putting it out. While he puts the village out, I tell him the story."

The interaction that came naturally with putting out Christmas decorations also gave Ellen the opportunity to share her Christian faith with her grandson. She said,

> I found that he loves window clings, so I bought some of the nativity. Every time he came over during the

holidays, he decorated the windows. I wanted him to know the Christmas story and give him other things to play with, so I bought a children's plastic play nativity. One day he pointed out to me, "Here's the mommy. Here's the daddy. Here's the baby Jesus in his car seat." One time he said, "And, oh, he needs his butt changed." Then he picked up the angel and said, "The fairy can do it." That gave me the opportunity to tell him about Christmas. Every time he came over he had to play with the set and get his Legos out to make little characters. He would place them around the nativity set and say, "That's so they can all look at baby Jesus." Christmas really did come alive again because this little guy was experiencing it.

Another holiday that Ellen loves is Easter. She said, "I'm the Easter egg person, and I always do the hunt. Last year I filled about 500 Easter eggs and hid them all over the yard and hanging from trees. Dillon came and brought his friends, and some other kids were invited, too. It was so much fun watching him and the others running all over our yard, picking up eggs. The holidays came alive again." Because Ellen was willing to share and go to the trouble of providing a fun time, she discovered a rewarding new way to interact with her grandson.

Other special events also give grandparents opportunities to forge bonds with their grandchildren. Leslie makes an effort to attend events for the grandchildren near her and to do things that will connect her with them. She said,

> I always go to Grandma Day at school, and I have books for them, and I read to them. I've even read Harry Potter because one of the kids was reading it, and I wanted a connection with her. I always remember

> their birthdays and Christmas with gifts. I have a rule that I spend about thirty dollars on each kid, maybe a little over or under, and they know to expect that. Our biggest family tradition is our Sunday dinners. Not everyone comes every week, but they're welcome. The kids think it's fun to play with cousins. We also have a boys' night and a girls' night every once in a while, and we try to make it special so they look forward to it.

Notice how important it is for the grandchildren to know what to expect and look forward to.

Sharon said that grandparents' attention is very important. She said, "Go often to sporting events, recitals, cook-outs, etc. Yell for your grandchildren, wear the t-shirt with their names, they will never forget it, they love it and love you for showing up."

Mitzi, as a grandmother and a step-grandmother, said, "We treat every one of them like our own family. We go to all of their events. Christopher's children are very musical and involved in theater and such so we go to lots of those events. They don't think of me any different from their other grandmothers because I go to their events." Mitzi is viewed the same as the other grandparents because she makes the effort to go to their special events.

I have found that my grandchildren even enjoy seeing me at their sibling's games so they have someone to sit with. Then I get the opportunity to ask them about their lives while we cheer for a brother or sister. The fact that I make such an effort gives me opportunities that I wouldn't have otherwise.

Diane and Randy also make an effort to go to the things their grandchildren do, as well as host events for the family, including their grandson's half-sister, Emma. Diane said,

> At the first of the season, Bridget (ex-daughter-in-law) would send us both kid's game schedules. We

go to all the kids' games, even Emma's games. As all our grandchildren got older and lived in other towns, we had games to go to all over the place, so we didn't try to go to all of them anymore. At the games, we would sit by their parents, even Bridget and her husband, Greg. Holidays we also spent together. Bridget would invite us to birthday parties for both kids. Because Bridget had plans for the children on Christmas and stuff like that, we never saw the kids on the day, so we gave gifts to the kids and a family gift on another day to make it special. In our family, we celebrate all the birthdays on the third Sunday of the month, so Riley and Emma would be here for those events, too.

Diane and Randy's daughter, Ashley, and her family participated in the events, as well. She said,

When Riley and Emma lived here, they were included in everything the family did, mostly just Riley and Emma, not Emma's other siblings, because they were too young. But we all made an effort to be in Riley's life. My parents tried to be there at least once a week and extended that to Emma. I considered ex-daughter-in-law, Bridget, part of the family, and I still do. I give them cards and such. We have the attitude that family is what you make it. Bridget even had a family portrait made, and she gave a copy to my parents. We all just make one big family.

Ashley said something very wise—family is what you make it. Notice that making something requires time and effort. Time and effort pay huge dividends in showing children you love them. Christopher said, "Remember your grandchild's birthday and write them special notes to congratulate them. Take notice of their accomplishments. They will treasure the attention they get from you."

Christopher really appreciates what all of his parents and stepparents do for his children. Ed and Ann make the holidays and special traditions meaningful for the children. Ann said,

> Ed always grows a garden. We'd grow pumpkins, and at Halloween the kids would pick out a pumpkin, and we'd spread out newspapers, and we'd carve the pumpkins. It was a mess, but they had fun. We made cookies for Christmas, and we'd decorate them, or for Valentine's or Halloween. Other times when we'd get together, we would play charades, but they mostly liked to hear stories about us as children. Ed is a great storyteller. They'd ask us to tell them the story of [fill in the blank] and we'd tell them. We had other traditions, too. We had a huge willow tree in our back yard, and the children would go out and sit under it and have popsicles. We'd call it the Popsicle Tree. We also had a trampoline that the kids liked to play on.

Christopher's stepmother, Mitzi, said,

> Dick makes sure that they have time at our cabin and for birthdays and graduations, and he goes to a lot of effort and makes it special. When it comes to holidays, we say to our children and grandchildren, be with the family you feel good about. I say you don't sulk and say you have to be here for Thanksgiving or Christmas. You can't mandate that. I'm sure there are times that are not totally comfortable, but I can't think of any because everyone tries to make our times together really pleasant. Dick had to learn to trust me

with his children that I wouldn't say it was his child or my child who did this or that. He learned that I had their best interest at heart, and he relaxed. He had to learn that just a little bit.

The lesson to be learned here is that it takes time to establish relationships, but that time and effort and attitude can make all the difference.

However, combining families and various traditions was not always easy or successful for Ed and Ann. Ann said,

> When we got married, his children were all grown, and most of them were married and had their own families. When Ed and I went on vacation it was usually just Christopher and my daughter and maybe his daughter. We went to Mexico and Lake Powell and other places, and that worked out OK. We tried to just combine the families. But his family was so much older they weren't involved with us as much. Our family was centered around family, and his wasn't that way. We tried to combine Thanksgiving and Christmas, and sometimes it worked and sometimes it didn't. His children were raised completely different from my children. Their mother was extremely strict and didn't let them have friends. My children had friends over all the time. It was like they were on a different planet from my children. It wasn't until adulthood that they could interact. I brought over Christmas traditions for our family. I tried having both mixed families over on Christmas day for breakfast, but the families didn't mix well. Eventually, it just ended up with my family. We tried to combine the families, and it didn't work too well.

The fact that Ann and Ed realized when something wasn't working is important. Even with the best of intentions, we can't force people to behave as we want them to. Ideally, everyone would get along, but when that doesn't happen, it's fine to gracefully discontinue something that makes everyone uncomfortable.

Another important principle is that grandparents can interact on these special days in their own unique ways. For Diane and Randy, it was sleepovers and going to the park. For Leslie, it was Grandma Day and Sunday dinners. As Christopher said, "My children benefit differently from each set of grandparents. The common denominator is that if grandparents invest in a child's life by being there and paying attention to him or her, there are tremendous dividends, in that the child will watch and listen to the grandparent."

In Christopher's family, Ann and Ed have their own traditions, and Mitzi and Dick have theirs. They play to their strengths and don't worry about what they can't do. For instance, Mitzi said, "They don't look forward to my cooking because I don't look forward to my cooking. But I write them notes and write them letters about what I notice that is really nice or if they had a hard time. That's my thing that I do."

Speaking of her step-grandfather's interactions with her children, Lily said,

> My kids love Grandpa. He plays in the snow with them, and he tells them to do naughty things to their mom. He is British, so we have a lot of family traditions that come from him. We used to go to England every year to visit him, but now that I have three children, that's harder. He tells all these stories of naughty things he used to do when he went to boarding school. He's the kind of grandpa that lets us do whatever we want, so I'm surprised we made it. The other

grandpa, the one living with us, thinks my children are the light of his life, and they love his approval and attention.

Notice that although the grandfathers have different personalities, they both have valued roles in their grandchildren's lives. Having defined roles in the family is important because it allows children to rely on relationships and understand that people can be different and still be worthwhile.

Many of the interactions between family members center on traditions that can have tremendous impact on family relationships. For example, Stan said,

> After my cabin was built, it became a family tradition to have everyone there a couple of times or more in the summer. It became a tradition for us to visit a souvenir shop at the end of the trip on the way home. The kids got to know what was in the shop and how much I was willing to spend on each one, so they planned for days about what they would get—just little trinkets, but it gave them something to remember our trips by. When my daughter divorced, it was even more important to continue the tradition. Her children felt alienated from the family, and visits to the cabin gave them a chance to interact with their cousins and feel like they belonged.

There are many ways for grandparents to show their interest. Caleb makes sure that his step-grandchildren know he is invested in their lives by recording events.

> I keep a journal, and I like to take little videos, and I like to remember them at all stages of their lives. I try to write little things about their lives, since I'm a

writer. I always write in my journal in church, and I have a collection of handprints that they like to look at, because they like to have me use a pen to outline their hands. To me, the most memorable thing is teaching Xander to read. I love to have little kids fall asleep in my arms. When I watch the videos, I burst into tears. You never get those moments back.

Leslie also feels it is important to record events with her grandchildren through pictures. As told in a previous chapter, she said, "I take pictures of us making cookies together and doing other things together so they will know that we did these things, even if they don't actually remember the event. They can look at those pictures after I die and remember that they did things with me."

Tom and Deirdre feel it is important to go to the children's events and to take pictures. Tom said,

> From the very beginning, we went to as many of the kids' games and concerts and plays as possible. Often we were the only grandparents there, so our presence meant a lot. Sometimes not even the parents could go. I remember the smiles when a kid got done and realized we were there. The hard part, besides scheduling, was to get them to remember to tell us when these things were happening so we could go. A couple of months after our son remarried, our new granddaughter provided us with a schedule of her basketball games, so we went to most of them. She saw us cheering for her on the sidelines, and I think that went a long way toward making her feel comfortable with us.

Deirdre said, "I even take pictures of them in their plays or games and post them on Facebook. The older kids are my Facebook friends, so they see when I post things. They don't say much about it, but I think they know I think they're special when I do that."

Being supportive grandparents is good for the children. Caleb explained,

> We try to be as supportive as possible. Everyone is invited to a birthday party. We have an open door policy. The exes and spouses are welcome in this house. It's their event, and we try not to exclude anyone. That's nonsense. My wife from the very beginning said it was no good to try to hurt the exes because it just hurts the kids. They need adults who can show how to be married happily. You can't have a bitter house. You just can't.

Bethany lives far from her step-grandchildren, but she feels it is important to let them know that she and her husband care about them. She also said that her efforts as the step-grandmother have improved her husband's relationship with his children, especially since he was absent from their lives much of the time as they were growing up. She said,

> If I was living closer I would go to the grandchildren's performances, but I'm not around most of the time. I usually send them birthday presents or a card for Valentine's Day or for Easter. Unfortunately, with more of them, I do it less. I at least send them a card or some kind of little thing for special occasions, especially since my husband never remembered to give them gifts before we were married because he's a guy. It's my way of getting them to have a better rela-

tionship with their dad. I give them things from both of us, and we've just kept it going with the grandkids. I make him sign the things we give them or talk to them on the phone. Otherwise he wouldn't say anything to anybody. It has results. His daughter said that now she has such a better relationship with her dad, and she doesn't see him any more than before, and so she doesn't know why it's so, but I know.

Angela tries to go to events and has special parties for her very diverse family. She said, "I wanted to be a grandparent like my parents. They loved their grandchildren and thought they were the greatest things on earth. They had traditions that brought the family close. I don't have all their traditions, but I do try to do some."

Angela made a huge effort over a long period of time to get to know her adopted grandchildren, and that effort has paid off. She said,

> For years, as they were growing up, I took each one of them out for their birthdays, and we would spend the whole day together doing whatever they wanted. In the summer I took them out to have adventures. We went to the zoo and museums, and when that wasn't a good enough adventure, we went to more interesting places, like the planetarium. One time after we had gone to the planetarium, Josh went with his school the next week, and he knew what was happening and could tell the others. He liked that. Their family also liked to go deer hunting, so I had them come after the hunt to my house where I would make them treats, and we would stay up late and watch videos and tell stories. I think they felt comfortable in my home because they would come over so often

to visit or feed the horses. One time, the youngest girl was at a horse event, and she fell off her horse and had to go home. She had them bring her to my house. She climbed right in my bed, so I sat on the bed with her, and we watched TV together.

Many special events and holidays are centered on food. Food means warmth and comfort and the fact that someone cared enough to spend time making it for the family. Often the kind of food served reflects a family's ethnic background or nationality or recipes handed down from generation to generation. Such dishes bring continuity and a sense of belonging to a family. Food often triggers good memories of specific people. Food is also a physical manifestation of the love and effort put into a get-together, and when people eat it, they are taking part in the love put into it.

For Shelley, certain foods bring back memories of her grandmother. She said, "Gram made sure we remembered and celebrated birthdays and special occasions. She made this angel food cake with cooked frosting that was amazing. No one since has made one that good."

Cathy also remembered her grandmother's food: "My grandfather would putter around and my grandmother would bake and cook pies—not cakes—pies. She'd get up super early and bake pies. I loved going to her house. Now I bake pies. I'm a very good pie maker."

Caroline is not comfortable as a cook, but she's learned how to cope and make dinners that her family enjoys. She said, "I can never get everything cooked and on the table at the same time. I mean, I would try to have mashed potatoes and rice and fried chicken and rolls with all the fixings," she said.

> I used to stress over that, and then my daughters-in-law kind of rebelled at all the starches and fried

> foods I was serving. Well, we'd been poor when I was growing up, and that's what we could afford. They were trying to get their husbands to eat more vegetables and fruits, so they suggested that I just cut up fresh veggies and fruits and keep the cooked foods to a minimum. That solved my problem. Now I just take things out of the refrigerator and have one or two cooked things, and everyone exclaims over how good it is.

For years, Deirdre, like Leslie, has had the tradition of hosting a Sunday dinner for the family. She said,

> My grandchildren love my cooking and love coming to dinner at our house. There are a few dishes that my grandchildren love and have become my signature dishes. When I went back to school, my grandson, who was only about six, said, "Nana, if you give your teachers your stew, they will all give you A's." My son's ex-wife did not like to cook, and I was happy to give her a break and do the cooking once a week. When my son remarried, I had to shift my thinking a little. His new wife is a good cook and wants to have us over for Sunday dinner sometimes, so we trade off now. It was important to validate her place in the family. I mean, I like to cook, and some of my own identity is tied up in being a good cook, but I can give that up and let her be the good cook, too. However, I knew I was making progress with my new step-granddaughter when she told me after one of my Sunday dinners, "Why don't you just come to our house and be our chef." I hope her mother didn't hear that.

Lily's blended family is also a blend of various food traditions. "My grandmother is a great cook. My mom, too. They're from British Guiana [now Guyana], so they cook good curry and roti (Indian flatbread). I love roti. Grandpa Dave can only boil potatoes." Of her other step-grandfather, she said, "My grandpa is the cook in that family. He makes good omelets. That's something we all remember."

In Dolores's family, meals were often hearty German fare. She said,

> My parents were from Germany and had suffered a lot of hardship, so they loved having huge dinner parties where everyone in the family came and there was a lot of food. We sometimes had over thirty people sitting down to dinner. I remember the smells and tastes of rotkohl (red pickled cabbage), sauerkraut and pork, boiled potatoes, and sometimes we had pflaumkuchen (plum and streusel cake) or chocolate covered German marzipan. We ate and ate and talked and laughed and laughed and laughed. Those were jolly times.

So food can be the vehicle for jolly times. When stomachs are full from good food, tensions are often eased, and people become more comfortable physically, which can make them more comfortable around the rest of the family.

Food is also a way to share a heritage. When Christopher was a boy, his stepfather shared his background in a way that has carried down to his step-grandchildren. Christopher said,

> My stepfather introduced to me to food that I love to this day, and my children love it, too. Biscuits and gravy. They ate it on the ranch, and that is something you can eat at 4:00 a.m. and it sticks with you. He taught me to make it. It's a real, rural ranch-folk food. My

kids and I eat it as a family. We never would have had it if he hadn't introduced us to it. We have hot cakes and call them that because that's what he calls it. He calls oatmeal "mush," and I say "Eat your oatmeal, but Grandpa calls it 'mush'" and we laugh about it.

Of his step-grandmother's influence, Christopher recalls, "My step-grandmother bottled everything. The first time in my life I had bottled meat was with her. She bottled deer meat, and it was really, really good, so my mother started bottling more because of her. My wife and I bottle now, but we don't bottle meat."

Food is often associated with a person. Sharon said,

Most of my memories with Grandmamma involved food. She made these big southern breakfasts with homemade biscuits, country ham, stewed apples, eggs, and pan-fried potatoes. I just loved the smells of food at her house during my summer vacations, which is usually when I visited after we moved out. I remember her in pastel-colored housedresses, cooking and humming.

Notice that the image of her grandmother is tied up with the wonderful food she served. Remembering the food brings back memories of Sharon's grandmother.

Bethany also carries on the tradition of cooking food her grandmother cooked. She said, "I make German pancakes that are like crepes like my grandmother made, not what some Americans call German pancakes. I still make those and popovers with melted butter and jam hot from the oven. The family really loves those." She remembers one food-related time when she was a child and her grandmother had all the granddaughters over for a sleepover. She said, "She made German pancakes for all of us and one of my cousins insisted she could eat as many pancakes as my grandmother could make. Each pancake was the size of a large skillet. My cousin ate eleven of them."

Roslyn's food is a large part of her relationship with her grandchildren. She said,

> We have been very involved in our grandchildren's lives. Even Tim, who is twenty-nine, is still involved with us. He thinks of our house as home. He comes in and says, 'Anything to eat?' He just goes through the refrigerator. We never had leftovers when he lived with us. He says nobody cooks such delicious food as his grandmother.

Notably, Tim connects being able to eat his grandmother's cooking with a sense of home.

Leslie started a food tradition when her sons were young:

> I made cookies for them every day so they would have warm cookies right out of the oven when they got home from school. My boys told me later that they loved the cookies. I liked it because I knew they'd always come home from school for the cookies, and while they ate them they would talk to me. One son said he always knew that there would be his mom with warm cookies when he came home. It was a great blessing for them. Now I make those cookies with the grandchildren. They call them "Grandma's Special Cookies." They don't know that I also give them to other people. They just think I make the cookies especially for them.

Angela had to integrate her adopted daughter's children into her home when Brenda's marriage disintegrated, and that included getting them used to the food she cooked. She said,

> I taught them to like the bean soups that I make. We made cupcakes like my parents' housekeeper used to make with a V-shape cut out of the middle and filled with raspberry jam and topped with whipped cream. I taught the girls how to make homemade bread, and I taught them to like my fudge. Most people make fudge and cut it into little pieces, but I spread it out on a platter and put it in the refrigerator. Everyone uses a spoon to just scoop up a bite when they want. The family makes patterns or roads in the fudge. My daughter makes flowers and loops—very pretty little patterns. My son makes streets. They had to get used to that. Now they like my food. The youngest girl is married with children now, and she invites me to go with them to church things and to birthday parties and such, and I share the things they've come to love.

Angela's food traditions helped smooth the way for the family to bond together, and that resulted in establishing family ties that have lasted through the years.

When I asked my friends what foods their grandparents made that they loved, the question was greeted with enthusiasm. It seems that memories of food associated with grandparents evoke strong feelings. Here are some of their answers:

> Homemade chicken noodle soup! With homemade egg noodles.

> My grandma could fry up a steak in butter like nobody's business!

> The German pancakes were a treasure. And the bowls of her raspberries!

My Grandma B made the best chili sauce.

I'm partial to my great-grandmother's bread.

My granny makes the best stew, but there's not a whole lot of her left anymore. . . . Sorry I just had to say that. On a serious note my granny makes the best biscuits and gravy.

My grandpa made poached eggs on toast. I know it ain't much, but to a ten-year-old kid, it was gourmet. I can't eat them without being transported back to his tiny kitchen.

Either her lasagna or her sausage dip! Both of them ruled. . . . I don't remember my "other grandma" making me any food. I remember cold water in aluminum tumblers at her house, though.

I loved my grandma's raisin-filled cookies. There were no kids in our family that hated raisins.

Pies, bread pudding, candies, oatmeal cookies with chocolate chips *and* raisins. . . . You get the picture.

Grandma used to make the *best* scrambled eggs. Ever. Even if they were dripping with cheese and butter.

My grandma made the best apple pudding with caramel sauce. I've tried to make it, but it doesn't quite taste like hers.

Rolls!

Cherry pie with tart cherries from her backyard.

Maternal grandmother: Parker House Rolls; Paternal Grandmother: Gooseberry pie.

Sometimes, though, grandchildren can be picky eaters. Ellen found that her oldest grandson will only eat certain things. She said,

> He lives on macaroni and cheese and applesauce. I always offer him something from our meal, but he just eats macaroni and cheese and applesauce. I also keep goldfish crackers around for him, because he will eat those. What I did with my son when he was growing up was to have one dish at a meal that he would eat, and I do that for my grandson, too. He will learn to eat other things when he gets older.

What her grandson is learning from having his grandmother accommodate his tastes is that she loves him and is more concerned about him than making him fit with what she wants him to do.

Food is time and effort and a physical manifestation of love that touches on most of the senses. Good food alleviates hunger pains, but more importantly, when it is associated with emotional ties to other people, it is one of the strongest memory-makers available. Traditions that involve food, as well as interactions between loved ones, can reassure family members that they are included and worthwhile. Pleasant memories encourage future involvement in family traditions, especially if people know they will be fed with love and good food.

Chapter Eight

Politics, Religion, and Other Times to Shut Up

We all have our opinions, but there is a time and place to share them. We all certainly have the right to free speech, but we also have the right to walk away from anything we don't like. Children and grandchildren will do just that. Stan said,

> I used to think it was my duty to set my grandchildren straight, and I'm afraid I lectured them on what they ought to be or do. My oldest daughter said something that changed me. She said, "You can't have any influence on someone who isn't there." She meant that I was driving the kids away and they didn't want to come to visit me. So I stopped the lectures. After our younger daughter's divorce, when we finally got to see her children again, I tried to just be positive with

them, so they'd like being with us. Same with her new stepchildren.

I had a similar experience. One time when I was bemoaning something one of my grandsons had done, my son said, "Don't let him hear you say that, or it will be a reason why he might walk away from you." Lesson learned—I never brought up my feelings about what he'd done, and our future interactions were much more pleasant.

Time and place and circumstances are important when delivering our opinions. Stan did not have a custodial role, but Shelley's grandmother did, and her influence shaped Shelley's life. Shelley said,

> My fraternal grandmother, "Gram," came to help when my youngest sister was born. My mother died unexpectedly, so my grandmother stayed for the next eight or nine years, acting as our surrogate mother. She was a strict disciplinarian, but we knew she loved us, and she was there when no one else was. She taught me values and morals, taught me how to work hard, and instilled in me high standards for whatever I did, including homework or whatever I was assigned to do.

Since Shelley's Gram assumed the role of parent, it was her duty to teach the children what a parent would teach. Just as parents each have their own style of parenting, grandparents have their own style as well. Shelley said,

> Gram was a staunch Republican and even had me type a letter to President Jimmy Carter letting him know that wearing a sweater while speaking to the American public was not acceptable. She was a Pres-

byterian because that's the church Scottish people went to. Not that she was Scottish, but her husband was, so that's where she went. We ate oatmeal for breakfast instead of cold cereal because any idiot knows that oatmeal is better. We went to church each Sunday in our pretty dresses, sat on the pew bench, didn't talk, and didn't color on the bulletin. No trips to the bathroom were allowed. End of discussion. There was no point in arguing, you weren't going to win.

Shelley accepted what her grandmother demanded, because she knew that her grandmother loved her and wanted the best for her.

However, as children get older, they don't *have* to stick around anymore, and they may not choose to listen. Conflict over differing opinions can be divisive. Sharon said, "It can be a source of conflict when the children/grandchildren choose a different religious path. Discussion of politics should be limited when grandparents and children/grandchildren have different political views." Instead of pontificating, Sharon's grandparents did something better to get their beliefs across. She said, "I remember that my grandparents always dressed neatly and expected us to do the same. They took us to church and on road trips to Detroit and Kansas City." It was natural for Sharon to go places with her grandparents. They made going to church just one of many places they went together.

Diane and Randy also took their grandchildren to church with them while raising them, and the children are still religious. Diane said, "Their mother was in the church, even though she had bad times, so we took them to church with us. We knew that was what she wanted."

GRANDPARENTING THE BLENDED FAMILY

We often behave the way our own grandparents treated us. Melanie, who has custody of her own granddaughter, explained how her grandmother influenced her:

> My grandmother was very well read and very knowledgeable about politics. I also am an avid lover of knowledge about politics. Religion is Episcopalian. I was baptized in this church, confirmed, an alter guild, baptized my children, too. I love the traditional aspects of this church and the leanings towards more thinking, intellectual followers. I don't believe in blindly following anything or making decisions based solely on emotions (not meaning that I have never done so . . . ha), and I share that with my granddaughter.

Ellen has had so much conflict in her life, after being raised with an alcoholic stepfather and the abuse that came from such a situation, that she tries very hard not to make difficulties in her grandchildren's lives. She said, "Our family doesn't have a lot of conflict. We all agree that we want to give these little guys the best environment, and that means no arguing." From her own experience, she has realized how harmful it can be for grandchildren to experience the conflict that can come from trying to blend a family with members who behave very differently. She said, "I was raised in a blended family, so maybe I'm more aware of how hurtful it is to see how the other grandparents treat stepsiblings. So I hope I don't replicate those feelings. They notice. The sad fact of the matter is that children pick up on feelings and emotions, regardless of actions. There are some things you can't help."

Ellen also tries to reduce conflict—even when she feels strongly about something, such as religion. She said,

> I'm very religious. I have a strong faith, and I'm dedicated to my church and living my faith. My daughter

was raised in that environment, but she does not share my consistency in that. Her husband is not at all—his folks stopped going when they got married because they were both raised in different religions. So sometimes my daughter wants to have some religion, but he doesn't, and there is conflict, which isn't good for the grandchildren. My mother is a United Methodist pastor, so my daughter wanted her baby son christened by her grandmother. Everyone came. Even my son-in-law and his parents came. Everyone was very moved.

Even with the lovely experience of the christening, Ellen found that her daughter's spouse and his attitude influenced her daughter away from being involved in religious activities. Soon after the christening, her daughter stopped going to church. Ellen said,

> My husband said to her, "You can have your son christened, but if you don't keep it up, it won't make any difference." Even what my husband said didn't make much difference. Now my daughter sleeps in on Sunday, and that bothers me. I want to nag her because it's my job as a Christian, so I make comments here and there. Most of the time she agrees and doesn't do anything. That is something I cannot force. It's their prerogative, so when Dillon is with me he knows who I am and that it's important to me. It's hard for me because I feel strongly that they need to be in a Christian environment with support from Christian friends with companionship and support and interaction. They just go, "Yeah, yeah," and do nothing.

But not interfering is as important as giving support. Ellen learned a valuable lesson about the difference. She said,

> It's hard to keep your mouth shut. I feel like I've learned so much and made so many mistakes, and I had no family around, so I want my grandchildren to benefit. Many times I have stepped in, like when I decided my daughter's house wasn't clean enough for my grandson, so I hired somebody to clean her house and even clean out the air ducts. That went over well. However, my daughter will call and ask for advice. I have found out that if I insert myself, it doesn't work so well. If she calls at her wits end, then I can step in. I have to be the peacekeeper and remind her that she has a gorgeous little guy.

In Caroline's family, politics is a source of contention that she and her husband have learned to leave alone. She said,

> We love listening to Rush Limbaugh and other political commentators like him. But not all of our family agrees with what those people say, and there have been some heated discussions at family get-togethers. My husband likes to lay down the law, but after a couple of huge arguments, even he has learned not to say too much. Some of the grandchildren are old enough to shoot us down when we quote Rush, and they're not afraid to speak their minds. We've kind of learned to keep our political opinions to ourselves and talk about other things.

Bethany has an opinionated husband, which causes some controversy. To avoid conflict, she has learned to tread softly when she is with her stepchildren and grandchildren. She said,

> We don't talk about anything controversial. Everybody is just pleasant. It's better to avoid it, but my

husband is very outspoken, so everyone just rolls their eyes when he starts on something. But me, I don't bring up anything. My husband does, though. He will get them all hopping pretty fast, and it's not good.

Keeping the peace is important to several of the people I interviewed. They feel that peace is better than being right. Once again, if the atmosphere in the family is unpleasant or contentious, no one wants to be together. With extended family, being together is more of a choice than a requirement, and people will simply choose not to be a part of something that is not appealing.

Tom and Deirdre, while religious themselves, have taken the position that they should be encouraging if a child, grandchild, or step-grandchild decides to go to church, but they don't argue with them about religion or politics or anything. Deirdre said,

> We try to be a positive influence in their lives, as well as non-judgmental. If one of them comes to us with questions, we answer them, but we don't try to push our opinions on any of them. It has brought about some interesting situations. For example, one teenage grandson became very upset with his mother, who had divorced his father, our son. He was upset because she started hanging out in bars and smoking and having an affair with some guy. She wasn't acting how he thought a mother should act—especially not his mother. He asked us to take him to McDonald's so we could just talk. He really unloaded on us about his mother's behavior and what he believed was right and wrong. He was deeply hurt by her behavior. He said that when he'd confronted her about her behavior, she'd told him that she wanted to act that way, and he should just get over it. He was confused. He

> wanted to be a good kid and go to church and do well in school, but his mother thought that was a waste of time. We were trying to be supportive of him without dictating anything or saying anything judgmental about his mother, but he came out and asked us our opinions. Very carefully, we said that we thought that he would be happiest if he tried to be the best he could, and that church and school were good things. That was so hard. Afterwards, my husband wanted to go knock some sense into that woman, but we held our peace.

There's that word again—peace.

Extended family relationships can be especially difficult to deal with. Ellen had to think hard about how she should be as a grandparent, and in-law. She said,

> Once the children are born, the in-laws take on a whole new role in my mind. Before the children came along, my role was to support my daughter and son in their relationships with their spouses. I felt defensive about my children. There were times when I would have supported them walking away from their marriages. But then a grandchild comes along and that in-law is my grandson's daddy or mommy. I went through a divorce when I was young, and I became aware of the negative effects of what my ex said to my kids, and I saw that it undermined my children's security. My job is now to support that relationship so my grandchildren are secure in their relationships with their parents. And that's sometimes hard. Especially about not going to church or not approving of their parents' work ethic. For instance, my son-in-law

> loves gaming, and I think he's creating a bad example for my grandson. There are times when I have to bite my tongue and not say what I want. I make sure that any interaction with the in-laws is positive. I know they both love their children, and my job is to support that. If there were any dangerous situations, my mouth would open in a hurry. That's the role of adults as protectors of children. When it came to opinions, though, my children and their spouses are the parents. What goes on in my house is different than in their home. All you can do is love them and be yourself. I keep looking at that book I read that said all they need is one strong example. Hopefully I can be an impact that way. What I learned from my children is to maintain a strong positive relationship with both their parents and help them be more mature and stable people. I almost view my role in that case as supporting them and making sure they know they're loved.

Ellen and several others voiced the opinion that it is important to be supportive and positive, rather than critical and nagging. Being positive and supportive will contribute to peace within a family. With all the turmoil in the world today, having peace in the family is a worthwhile goal.

When a family falls apart, grandparents can be a stable influence that allows children to form their belief systems just by being examples. Caleb said,

> I am closer to my grandparents than I ever was to my parents. I grew up next to them, and they taught me everything that I know. I've been estranged from my parents and brothers and sisters, but I do see my

cousins. My grandparents shared their testimony of the gospel with me and gave me unconditional love. It was my grandparents who I went to when I needed wisdom and financial help. It's my grandparents who taught me that love is sacrifice.

Sometimes the conflict isn't over religion or politics, but when to reveal disturbing information to the children. Diane and Randy are in a delicate position. Their son committed suicide, and they cannot tell their grandson how his father died. Diane said,

> Our son committed suicide after he'd divorced Bridget and then remarried. When my son died, his ex-wife Bridget didn't want Riley to know how his father died. She thought that my grandson wouldn't understand about depression, and if he saw his mother sad, he would worry that she might commit suicide, too. We let everyone in the family know it was Bridget's call when to tell Riley. Our son's second wife was in counseling after he committed suicide, and she said that it was better to know the truth and the other children should know the truth. So as other children in the family grow up, they are told the truth, but not Riley. So I told Bridget that the other children may say something because they knew, but it was her call as to when to tell Riley. However, I worry about what his reaction will be when he finds out.

Being able to tell grandchildren the truth is important for establishing trust. But the other part of trust is honoring the wishes of family members. It goes both ways. It is important that grandchildren have someone they can trust to tell them the truth about any number of things. The fact that grandparents are significantly older than grandchildren can mean that grandchildren view grandparents as being too old to know anything. If grandparents want children to listen to them, it is important to establish a give-and-take relationship with them. The grandchildren may know something grandparents don't, even little things, and if we let them teach the older generation, grandchildren will feel more comfortable listening as well. Gloria explained, "A vacation with my granddaughter and her husband and children is delightful. Grandson-in-law does the driving, granddaughter does the cooking, and I get to play with the kids, although a lot of the playtime consists of the little ones explaining to me how their electronic devices work."

Gloria is a great example of being willing to learn new things and allowing her grandchildren to teach her. I have seen many people who aren't willing to learn about new technology and how it creates a gap between them and the younger generation. Since technology is such a huge part of society now, being willing to learn new things—and being willing to learn those things from grandchildren—can help families feel more connected.

This give-and-take is very important. Christopher said, "It's important for the grandparent to be able to entertain opposing opinions or the child considers them old, inflexible, and out of touch. If they are able to entertain and listen to the opposing opinion, then the child considers the grandparent wise and able to weigh ideas and make choices. This is a far more important lesson."

Not all grandparents have to do things the same way. As mentioned before, Christopher also said,

> One unique thing about having step-grandparents and grandparents is that you have additional sets of "parents" who provide different examples of mentoring, discipline, and love. My children benefit differently from each set of grandparents. The common denominator is that if grandparents invest in a child's

life by being there and paying attention to him or her, there are tremendous dividends, in that the child will watch and listen to the grandparent.

Christopher makes an important point. You are not the same as any of the children's other grandparents, so you have your own unique way of influencing the family.

His relationship with his stepfather has had a huge impact on Christopher's opinions about religion that has influenced his beliefs as an adult about more than just religion. Christopher said, "The fact that I'm actively religious has a significant connection with my stepfather. He fought in WWII, but he was converted in the army. So he was adamant that we always go to church. If my mother said, 'Oh, let's not go.' He would say, 'If you don't go one time you won't go others.' It's the same thing with other things you try to learn, like piano or work."

It is interesting to note that each of Christopher's parents and stepparents view their role as advisor differently. One set of Christopher's parents, Ed and Ann, try very hard to tread lightly with the grandchildren. Ann said,

> It's good to give advice when they ask. The grandchildren sometimes come to us for advice. They will say, "What do you think I should do?" We always give them a little advice, but we say, "It's your decision. You have to make up your own mind." I'd like to interfere a lot of times, but I don't. Ed is more straightforward. He just says it like it is. He has this saying that I told him I'm going to put on his tomb: "If you can't do anything about it, don't worry about it." He says that to me. He's just very, very even tempered. I'm the one that flies off the handle. We just had a granddaughter come over the other day saying,

"I don't know what to do, I don't know what to do." We said, "You have to make the decision." You can't make a decision for your grandchildren. They have to learn how to make their own decisions. Because we don't tell them what to do, they feel good about coming to us.

On the other hand, Christopher's other set of parents have a slightly different role when it comes to giving advice. Mitzi said,

We do give advice. It just depends on what the children need. Lots of times they call for financial advice or if they want to use the cabin. Sometimes they call with husband and wife questions and what to do with the kids. Every once in a while I have to be careful with what I say. Our children let us be grandparents to all of the grandchildren. We don't try to discipline them or things like that. You really need to have a sense of humor and make things light. Don't make things out of nothing; that's not necessary.

In the culture of your family, you must carefully decide what will be the best way to deal with delicate topics like religion and politics. Julie has strong opinions, but she says she doesn't lecture, especially about religion, although she and her husband take the children with them to church if they are visiting. Julie said,

Religion is a must to a healthy child. They need to see the divine nature of God, the earth, and life. Our biggest pain has been the movement of our daughter into a so-so attitude toward our religious beliefs. But we see to it that our grandchildren attend meetings when we live close by. Thus, when they moved away, our reward was the children dragging the parents to

> church. My one granddaughter once introduced me as "the most religious person I know," and I am far from religious. But this moment defined one of the most important influences I had made in her life. Now I watch ever so carefully what I do. Those little stinkers are watching me!

Julie hit the nail on the head. Those little stinkers will watch you and what you do.

Mitzi had some especially good advice on handling differences of opinion. She said,

> In our family, we recognize that we have people who don't think like we do. We all have the right to our own opinions, but we don't argue. That just gets into fighting. I have found that if the fighting starts, that's not good. We have never had a fight start in our family. We don't fight over religion or politics. Children fight like normal children, but I have never been to one gathering where there has been fighting. We're not wishy washy, but we're all smart enough not to get on the topics where we disagree."

It would probably be a good thing if we were all smart enough not to cause dissension in our families.

Chapter Nine

Enriching Lives: When It's Time to Put Up and Speak Up

Divorce, illness, and death are tragic—but they are also expensive. They take a toll on family resources, complicating the use of both time and money. In the aftermath of such disasters, the family is often thrust into survival mode where things like piano lessons or Little League fall by the wayside. Enter the grandparents or step-grandparents like knights in shining armor with additional resources of time, experience, and, perhaps, money.

After her divorce, Lily's mother had to work and couldn't spend as much time with Lily. Her education could have been neglected, but Lily's grandparents and step-grandparents stepped in. They took an interest in enriching her life in several ways that extend into adulthood. Lily said,

> My grandpa living with me now taught me a love of everything I love now. He gave me the complete

works of Shakespeare in sixth grade and several other classics. He took me to the opera. He taught me about the power of myth and the works of Joseph Campbell. He taught me how to do crossword puzzles. Even though he's ornery on the outside, he's the kindest man ever. He's taught me more about service than anyone. While he lives with us, I never fold laundry. I don't empty the dishwasher or do gardening. He just likes to be useful and serve others. My other step-grandpa always helped me with my homework. He remembers things he reads. On another side of the family, my stepdad's parents are really young, in their 60s, and we go four-wheeling with them and do fun things in the outdoors. They also taught me about genealogy and family history.

Similarly, as a new step-grandparent, Caleb found himself with more of a parental role when his stepdaughter's boyfriend left her after she became pregnant. He has taken an interest in his step-grandchildren's education and other things as well. As mentioned before, he said of his first step-grandchild, "I was his parent as he grew up, and still, to this day, I sit down and do his homework with him; I taught him to read, and I cleaned up his vomit and changed his diapers."

Caleb learned to be a grandparent from his own grandparents. He said, "My grandparents taught me to love books. I want my grandchildren to be surrounded with books. I think that reading is a foundation for life. They also taught me to love work." He is also very interested in his step-grandchildren's education. He said, "My stepchildren let me pick the schools for the grandchildren because I pay for them. I put my money where my mouth is. I want them to feel that I am invested in them."

Caleb has an extensive garden, and he takes his grandchildren with him to help him work in it. He said, "All the grandkids go out in the garden and work. They do housework with me. They go out on my work with the newspaper with me. Xander thinks, to this day, that he works for the newspaper. Then he sees that this is how we pay the bills." But he doesn't just teach the children to work. He teaches them to have fun, too. For example, he said, "One time we built a zip line in the backyard, and the kids loved it." Caleb includes the children in his day-to-day activities, whether they are work or play.

When children are learning to perform and use their talents, they sometimes need someone to sit and appreciate them, which takes time that parents sometimes don't have. Giving approval and showing appreciation of whatever children are trying to do or learn is important and gives them the confidence to keep on trying. Myfanwy said, "Grandma and Grandpa are always happy for us to come over and sing to them and play the piano. That is a safe place to gain some confidence in our musical abilities."

Her husband, Sean, also remembers how good it was to have his grandparents interested in him. He said, "They came to my high school graduation. My dad's parents came to see me play in a jazz band at the university, and they liked it. I appreciated it."

Caroline loves to help her grandchildren grow. She said,

> I've taught many of the girls to knit and crochet. We go to their concerts and recitals for dance or singing or playing instruments and to their plays, and when they come to our house, we have them perform their parts or play their instruments for us. It is getting harder to get out and go to these events, but I'm always glad I do. The grandchildren love to see me there. Even the neighborhood children know that when they come to

my house for Halloween, they have to sing or say a poem for their trick-or-treat before I give them anything. Some of them practice all year because they know they will have to perform for me.

What a great blessing it is for these children to know that they have an interested and loving audience.

Sharon appreciated her grandmother's support, especially after her parents' divorce. She said, "My grandmother just loved me and praised me and told me how wonderful I am. She didn't worry about spoiling my cousins, brother, or me. I guess that's because she knew that our parents instilled discipline and set boundaries. She just made us feel like she enjoyed being with us as much as we enjoyed being with her."

Her other grandparents' influence also shaped Sharon's life. She said,

> My grandfather would give us little chores around the funeral home to keep us out of the way, and he paid us a few quarters. Usually, we would sweep the front walk, dust, run the vacuum. We would spend our earnings at the candy store down the block or Dairy Dip, a walk-up ice cream store that sold soft-serve vanilla ice cream cones. Everyone in the neighborhood knew that we were Will Henry and Annie's grandchildren, and that carried a certain amount of prestige because they were considered reputable and generous members of the black community.

Although Sharon's immediate family experienced hard times and her mother had to work hard at lower paying jobs, her grandparents gave Sharon the confidence to get an education. She earned a PhD and is now a member of the faculty at a university.

Gloria's experience taught her to treat her own children differently than she was raised. She said,

> I wish my mother had taught me to aspire to a higher education. Few in our large extended family had gone to any college at all, and none to a prestigious university. Back then, all those years ago, I had no one to guide me. My mother's mother had arranged that each of her eight daughters would learn a trade—seamstress, teacher, telegrapher, among others—so that they could be self-supporting, although all of them married at a time when husbands supported their wives. Today, all my daughters are professional women—a doctor, two engineers, a writer, a designer. I strongly urge my granddaughters to fortify themselves with careers that will serve them for a lifetime.

Because Gloria encourages her own children to aspire to greater things than she had the opportunity to accomplish, her grandchildren will have excellent examples of family members who succeeded in careers and getting an education. Gloria is another example of how a grandparent's actions will benefit future generations.

A grandparent can make all the difference when it comes to children realizing their potential. "It was important to make sure that our grandchildren's talents were fostered," said Stan. "We looked for ways to do it." Dolores added,

> We paid for piano lessons and singing lessons. We also paid for some summer camps where the emphasis was on things like art or music. We knew that with all the trouble happening in our daughter's life, she

> didn't have the money to pay for things like that, and our grandchildren's childhood was in danger of passing by without those advantages. As a result of us paying for her music lessons, when our oldest granddaughter wanted to go to the university, she got a scholarship in music. In fact, many of our grandchildren went to college on scholarships.

Tom and Deirdre make the effort to give their grandchildren and step-grandchildren experiences and opportunities, and their efforts are paying off in ways they hadn't really considered. Deirdre said,

> I guess I shouldn't be surprised that my two oldest grandsons and my oldest step-granddaughter are all involved in drama at their school, because we've taken them to plays and concerts over the years. So of course they'd be interested in performing. We've also gone to their concerts, plays, and sporting events. Their faces light up when they see that we are in the audience—that we're there to cheer for them and take pictures of them. I remember one time when our grandson had a concert and no one in the family could go but me. He seemed so grateful that I was there. After the concert, he walked shoulder-to-shoulder with me all the way out to the car, as if he was saying, "This is my Nana. See, everybody, I have someone who cares for me." It made me feel good.

Roslyn and Stephen took on the financial responsibility of raising their grandchildren when they took their grandchildren in, and that included school fees, athletics, and health care. Stephen said, "Braces. We paid for their braces. They were in braces for years." Roslyn said,

> When our grandson was in soccer, I went with him as long as he played soccer. Then Charlotte wanted to play, so I went to all the games. Charlotte and Jennie did swimming, and I went to all their meets. Going with them kept us younger than we would be otherwise. When Charlotte was in third grade, we got her into an arts academy. It's a regular school, but they would walk to the local theater and were introduced to the streetcars and buses and learned how to use them. There were so many life lessons she learned there. Charlotte was very good in painting and painted some wonderful pictures. One year, one of the parents bought one of her paintings in the art show for $25. That was against the rules, but the woman wanted it so badly that Charlotte gave it to her, and the woman paid her for it. Now we help her pay for college.

Angela also tries to help out her step-grandchildren as they go to college. She said,

> When it came time for the kids to go to college, I would give them each $100 a month, like my father gave his grandchildren. When the oldest girl wanted to go to college, she asked her mother, Brenda, if I would give her the $100 a month like I had to the others. When Brenda asked me, I said I would, but the girl had to come and talk to me about it herself. She did come, but she sat out in front of my house in her car for a long time, so I went out and asked her how she was and told her she was a good person to want to go to college. Then she came inside, and we had a good talk. She's married and has children of her own, one with special needs. He's a delightful little boy. I

told her she was a good mother, and she looked really surprised. With a little encouragement, she was able to go to college and improve her life.

Mitzi and Dick also try to contribute a little money to their grandchildren. She said,

> I don't necessarily do anything special, just grandmother things. I make quilts for different ones. I don't try to do things equal for each grandchild, but just with their personalities and likes and dislikes. About our only tradition is that when they turn 16 we give them $100 and hope they don't wreck their car on their birthday like one granddaughter did. They certainly do look forward to that $100 bill.

Grandparents today have the ability to offer more than the grandparents of yesterday. Tom explained,

> My grandparents always seemed aged to me. They couldn't move quickly, and their interests were very placid. On the contrary, I'm an intensely active grandparent. I've motorcycled for years, scuba and skin dived, bicycled, walked, and I still enjoy adventures like driving, sightseeing, and doing new and interesting things. Because of that, I have a great deal of interesting information and experiences to share with my grandkids, and I don't seem so old to them. Also, our age group in this day and age seems to be healthier and more fit than my grandparents did.

Christopher is grateful for what his grandparents and step-grandparents gave him. He said,

> Both sets of grandparents were committed to education. So I inherited books—literature, poetry, Browning, Dickens, the classics. Each, in his or her own way, introduced me to life lessons and what life has to offer, far beyond what I felt my parents provided. Whether it was books, travel, values, companionship, or love of learning, my grandparents encouraged me, through example and through giving, to take advantage of what life had to offer.

What Christopher's grandparents and step-grandparents did for him has also influenced his children. As mentioned previously, he said,

> One unique thing about having grandparents is that you have additional sets of 'parents' who provide different examples of mentoring, discipline, and love. My children benefit differently from each set of grandparents. The common denominator is that if grandparents invest in a child's life by being there and paying attention to him or her, there are tremendous dividends, in that the child will watch and listen to and learn from the grandparent.

Christopher's situation proves that the influence of grandparents and step-grandparents can go on for generations. He said,

> I intend to be a grandfather like my grandfather was, constantly interested in participating in their lives and telling them that they have the potential to be great. I also want to show them by my example that learning is a life-long objective and one does not have to waste one's years because he is old. I want to teach them that boredom is a matter of choice, not circumstance.

Deirdre also loves books and has passed that love to her grandchildren. She said,

> I keep a bookcase by the front door with new books appropriate for their ages. I kind of spend a lot on books. The children know that when they come to visit, they can take a book home with them and then return it next time they come and get a different book. The other night, we had a family party, and all the adults got busy talking. The little kids went down to the playroom, but the older kids really had nothing to do, and they weren't interested in joining the adults in our conversation. I glanced over at one point and saw all three of the older kids sitting on the floor reading some of the new books from the bookcase. I thought that was pretty good, especially because my oldest step-granddaughter used to not read much. Reading has helped them in school and has given them personal interests in subjects. My oldest grandson studies anything he can about World War II. His reading has improved his vocabulary to the point that he says his friends call him the professor. I think my books are a good investment in their future. I recently found from my oldest grandson that some of the books I lent him are among his favorites, and he kind of associates those books with memories of me.

Larry said that, in his family,

> It is all about sports. We go to our grandkids' games, and when the kids come over, we have a family football game or go to the park and play baseball. My wife gets after me all the time. She tells me to remember how old I am and, boy, did she let me have it when I

fell on the football and broke my ribs during the family Thanksgiving football game. It was still fun, and the kids love it, so I'll probably keep on playing.

My grandfather loved to get us interested in all kinds of scientific things. He was a doctor who taught at the university medical school, and he always wanted to share his knowledge with us. I remember one time he had the entire family go to dinner at a fancy restaurant where we ate the meal at a huge banquet table in a room that was separate from the rest of the restaurant. I clearly remember my grandfather standing at the head of the table explaining how to excise a cyst. I have to laugh at my grandmother's horrified expression as my grandfather explained how to slice open the skin over the cyst, being careful not to puncture the membrane around it, and how to lift it out—all explained as we were eating a nice meal. I especially remember the Jell-O and how it behaved in a rather cyst-like manner when I poked it.

What I especially liked about my grandfather was that he thought I was smart. He liked to invent things and held several patents. There was often some experiment or other going on in his house or in the large glass greenhouse he had in his backyard. I remember a time when he took me out to the greenhouse, where there were vats of algae, and explained to me his project that he was working on with a Japanese scientist to formulate the algae into tablets that could provide protein and other nutrients to people in third world countries. I was proud that my grandfather considered me intelligent enough as a child to understand his projects. He wanted me to become a medical doctor, which I seriously considered, but I got a PhD instead. I like to think he would be proud of me.

Travel is another way that grandparents enrich their grandchildren's lives. Roslyn is a German who transplanted to the United States and wanted to share her heritage with her grandchildren. She said, "We took the girls over to Germany to visit, and Charlotte did not want to go to Germany, to Hamburg, so we argued. She came with us and didn't want to leave Germany and wanted to go to school there, but we had to come home." Her granddaughters will remember sharing their grandmother's cultural heritage for a long time, and their own experience has been enriched.

Stan and Dolores took a granddaughter with them when they went to Disney World. Stan said,

> We wanted to go, but we were getting older, so we thought that maybe our sixteen-year-old granddaughter wouldn't mind being with old people, we could take her along to help us, since Dolores was in a wheelchair. We would give her a good time at Disney World, and she could help take care of us. She very graciously said she would, and we all had a great time. I think she enjoyed herself. At least she's smiling in all of the pictures.

Tom and Deirdre have taken grandchildren on motorcycle trips that their grandchildren still talk about. Deirdre also planned a trip based on their state's history that the entire family participated in. She said,

> I wanted the family to understand where we came from, since some of our ancestors helped settle this state. We drove from one historical site to the next. I had word and trivia games for them to do in the car between each site, and each child who completed the game got a prize, so that made them want to do the games. At each site, we learned a little lesson that lasted only a couple of minutes. The trip lasted two days, so I had us all stay at a motel with a nice indoor swimming pool, and the family had a great time. I think it went well.

Whether grandparents share interests, culture, fun experiences, or travel with their grandchildren, the sharing itself will strengthen family relationships and enrich the lives of all who are involved.

CHAPTER TEN

Going the Distance—When Families Are Far Apart

As I went down the hall at the university where I teach, I saw one of the secretaries sitting at her desk having a conversation with no one—at least no one whom I could see. She laughed and began singing a children's song. That's when I noticed the video on her computer screen of a little boy. I could hear him singing along with her. Later, I found out the secretary's grandson lived in Japan where his father was working and that she scheduled a computer visit with her grandson a couple of times a week. During their time together, she taught him songs they could sing together, read picture books to him, viewed pictures he'd drawn, watched him role play, and generally gave him her whole attention. She said that he loved the attention, and so did she. It was her way of sustaining a relationship with him that had begun when he was a baby living in the same town.

Many families live apart from each other, separated by physical distance, but that doesn't mean they have to be emotionally distant. The people interviewed for this book had strategies to close physical distance and maintain relationships. For instance, Gloria has embraced technology and uses it to communicate with her family. When it came time for Gloria's birthday, distance wasn't a problem:

> Yesterday was my birthday, and last night we celebrated together in a first-of-its-kind electronic family get-together. Daughter Lanie, daughter Laurie and her husband Andy, granddaughter Kathy and her husband D.J. and two little girls, granddaughter Kristin and her sweet kids—all were in their own homes at four different locations in Colorado. And daughter Joni was in Santa Fe. The only party people in our Boise house were daughter Jan and Ed and me. But we all could see each other and hear each other, and they sang Happy Birthday in a big family group. How'd we do it? Our total group has four iPhones and two iPads with the FaceTime app, and three computer screens with Skype. These were at the varying locations. By turning the screens with their built-in sharp cameras this way and that, everyone could see everyone else right in our Boise kitchen, even if only on small or medium screens. And it worked! Little Megan tried to blow out the candles on my birthday cupcakes—she could see them on her iPad screen in Colorado. Best of all, my husband set up our video camera on a tripod, so the whole long "I'm-here-and-you're-there-but-we're-all-together" party was video recorded. My husband and I watched it afterward on our big TV

screen, and it was great. What a cool birthday party! I want to do it again, and not wait for another birthday.

The electronic party was such a success that now Gloria and her husband use technology for other events. During her interview, Gloria said,

> Today is great-granddaughter Jessica's eighth birthday. Even though Jessica lives in Colorado and we live in Idaho, we were able to sing Happy Birthday to Jessica, who heard us and saw us across all those miles. Using the Apple iPad app called FaceTime, we were brought together so realistically that it felt we were close. When I turned eight years old seven decades ago, I got a long-distance phone call from my aunt in Pittsburgh. Long-distance calling was expensive, and we were barely coming out of the Great Depression. To make a call, my aunt had to ring the long-distance operator and tell her our phone number in Duquesne, all of eleven miles away. Do I love this new world where I can see and hear Jessica while I wish her a happy birthday? You bet I do!

Julie and her husband also use technology to stay in touch with their grandchildren. She said,

> There is no occasion that cannot be made better by having Grammie and Papo there. We attempt to get to every event, and when we can't, we ask for videos and pictures. We have stood in a crowded store watching phone videos of our grandchildren doing 'their thing' in school programs. We listen to choir concerts over the phone. Being there in any way possible to support them and watch them grow is so important.

Leslie has children and grandchildren scattered all over the country. Leslie said,

> Skype is a wonderful thing. We love getting together through Skype. Then when the kids see me, they don't think I look strange because they saw me just last week. We have little signals and secret words that they know. For example, we do that rubber chicken thing that the photographers do to loosen everyone up and make them smile. You know, like hitting ourselves over the head with a rubber chicken and saying something like, "Don't hit me, chicken." For some reason one little girl thinks that is hilarious and has for the last three years.

Ellen and her family also use Skype and cell phones to maintain family relationships over distances. She said,

> I really do think that what my aunt says is true—that we were meant to live in a village where extended family could be there. I think that village mentality is not always there because we are spread out all over the country, and that's too bad. So, I do Skype with them. The ones back East don't get it because they are too young. But when I am back East, I will Skype with my other grandchild. The first time we did it, my daughter and I got it all set up. My daughter turned the computer, so my grandson could see it from where he was playing on the floor, and she said, "Dillon, look who wants to talk to you on the computer!" He looked up and saw me on the screen and his little face just lit up. He ran toward the computer with his arms outstretched to give me a hug, and all I could see was his lips pressed up against

> the screen. Now he loves talking to me on the computer, and it's a really happy time for us. We even bought my son back East a computer so he could Skype with us. I sing with my grandson and tell him stories. Even cell phones are good. When my daughter picks up her son from day care and drives him home, it gets stressful trying to drive with a two-year-old in the car. My daughter will call me on her cell phone and tell me, "Your grandson wants to talk to you." Then she hands the phone to Dillon. We sing and talk all the way home. Technology is awesome.

Technology is awesome because it can make visible the love and effort grandparents put into their relationship with their grandchildren.

When Caroline's son married a woman who had a daughter, Caroline made sure to get her new stepdaughter's phone number. She said,

> I'm always amazed that kids have their own phones, but I'm sure glad they do. Even my step-granddaughter has one, and she's only twelve. She and I have talked several times on the phone, and I think she feels more comfortable with me every time I talk to her. I was hesitant at first about calling her. I mean, how would a twelve-year-old girl feel about talking to an old woman she barely knows? But I told myself to forget about myself and make the effort. I'm glad I did. She acts like she's happy, really happy, to talk to me, and she tells me about her life. I think she likes the attention. The funny thing is that the first time I texted her, she texted back, "Who is this?" When I

texted back that I was her Grandma, she was relieved I wasn't some stalker. Now she likes it.

Ed and Ann also stay in touch with their grandchildren through Skype and telephones. Ann said, "We stay very close to them. I call up and talk to one grandson and ask him about school, and we stay close. They tell us their problems and what they want to be and about school. We Skype with them and write them emails when we aren't close. We also stay in close touch with my husband's grandchildren through Skype and email."

Mitzi and Dick also use technology to stay close to the grandchildren. Mitzi said,

> Two of Dick's grandchildren live far away from us, and we're not on Facebook, so we do email and texting on the telephone. They come for weddings and things like that, and we go visit them. That's important. Dick has a daughter who is an artist, and we go every March to her show, and we really enjoy it. Dick is very close to my grandchildren, and they think he's wonderful.

Stan and Dolores are not as computer savvy as some, but they used a technologically based system—the U.S. Postal Service—in an unusual way to contact their grandchildren when their ex-son-in-law spirited the children out of state and they couldn't be found. It was Dolores's idea. She said,

> One of our granddaughters was having a birthday soon. I felt so sad because I didn't know where she was, and we were worried about her and the other children, especially because her father was a shady character. A few weeks earlier, we'd gone to their house with some jam I'd made for them and found it

> empty. There had been no sign that they would move, and we had no word from them afterwards. We were cut off. That was devastating. It was such a shock. We thought we had a good relationship with them, and then they disappeared without a word. What a cruel thing to do. And then it came to me—the Post Office probably had a forwarding address. I sent our granddaughter's birthday card with a check in it to her old address. When it was cashed, I had the bank trace the check and found out the town where they'd moved to, which turned out to be clear across the country. Then I got in touch with that town's records office and got an address because he had to take out a business license. Not long after, my daughter left him, but he kept the kids. It took a couple of years of negotiations with the ex, but we were finally able to establish regular visits with the kids. Now that they're grown up, they come to visit us on their own.

Other grandparents interviewed for this book also use the postal system, but mostly to send letters. Diane said,

> I've wondered what to do with Riley's family since they moved to Michigan. I'm not sure going forward. I have sixteen grandchildren and not all of them I see regularly. One of my granddaughters in California sent me a letter, so I wrote them all letters once a month so they could get something in the mail. Now that they've moved away, I include Riley and Emma and send them a letter every couple of weeks. It's kind of awkward because we're not related to the parents, so we don't talk on the phone. Riley really misses us, but I don't know if Emma does. She's

making relationships with the other grandparents. Riley had a cell phone, but he lost his, so mostly it's the letters.

Visits are an important way of strengthening relationships. Deirdre said,

> I feel so lucky that most of our grandchildren live close by. I saw how my children missed their grandparents when we lived several states away and my parents lived in California. My children remember when their grandparents flew them to Los Angeles and took them to Disneyland and Sea World. They knew that their grandparents didn't have a lot of money and had been saving up a long time to do it, so the kids really treasured that experience getting to know their grandparents. That was also the only time my parents could afford to do something so grand. The children took lots of pictures, and they loved the fact that they got to fly on a plane by themselves. Later, when we all moved closer to each other, the children had no problem being comfortable with their grandparents because they knew their grandparents cared about them and they had shared memories. Now I have a couple of guest bedrooms that my grandchildren know they can stay in when they come to visit. The bedrooms are familiar and part of our routine together.

One nice thing about letters and cards is that they are a tangible reminder of grandparent's love for their grandchildren. Because letters are not sent as often anymore because of email and texting, getting a letter is a unique event for a child that they appreciate. Caroline said, "I try to send cards and personal letters to all of my grandchildren. It makes my day when they send one back to me. It makes me feel like we have a connection."

Tom's grandparents also lived in another state. He said,

> My dad's folks we saw only when visiting Utah and that wasn't very often. However, I have very fond memories of my grandfather who was a real gentle man in every way. He had a fun but gentle sense of humor that we all thoroughly enjoyed. I just liked to be around him a lot as he always made me feel welcome and loved. My Nana was more business-like. We couldn't run or be a kid in her home because she had some nice things and didn't want them damaged. But she made fabulous dinners that we enjoyed when visiting. I do remember those visits with them.

Roslyn and Stephen's grandchildren all live away from them, but they maintain their close relationship through phone calls and letters and visits. Roslyn said,

> At Thanksgiving, they all end up here, except Jennie, who is in Washington DC. We were going to visit her at Thanksgiving, but the other kids all said, "You can't leave." They are so used to coming to us. So we told Jennie we are going to visit her between Thanksgiving and Christmas to keep everyone happy. Charlotte is going to college, but she is coming along on the trip to visit her sister.

As was mentioned in another chapter, Lily visited her step-grandfather in England. She said, "We used to go to England every year to visit him, but now that I have three children, that's harder." She feels it is important to maintain relationships, even though her own family situation is changing as her family grows in size and age. She said, "My grandparents gave me the travel bug, and I want my kids to have it, too. We'll try to go on more trips. It's important for the kids to know their grandparents."

Gloria's family also plans trips together. Recently they went on a trip to California. She said,

> This afternoon, we went to the beach. We parked the car very close to the beach, and I was able to take my walker through the sand with much help from my husband. It was really hard to move the wheels through the sand, but we got there. The kids had rented a beach umbrella and four little beach chairs. The little ones went down to play in the waves, and I stayed seated the whole time on my walker and just enjoyed listening to the ocean and watching the waves, so much that after a while I fell asleep. The little kids took a box of crackers and kept throwing crackers to the seagulls. They loved watching the gulls rush forward to grab the crackers. When we came back to the room, Kristin made a wonderful dinner of tacos. This was a great day, and tomorrow we're going to Disneyland.

Ed and Ann decided to take their grandchildren on a once-in-a-lifetime cruise. Ann said,

> We took several of the kids on a cruise, and we had a wonderful time. The ship's crew caught one little one wandering the aisles where we were staying, and he was saying, "I'm trying to find my grandpa." We were glad to get him back. We just had fun with them on the cruise ship. One grandson keeps asking, "When are you going to take us on another cruise?" So I guess they had a good time, too. Of course, we

can't afford to do that all the time. It was fun watching them, though. We got pictures to remind us all of what a good time we had, and we look at those.

Trips can be a wonderful time to get to know each other, and they don't have to be long. I remember that my grandfather organized a day trip every year on Memorial Day. The family gathered from various states, so it was also a reunion. All year long, he scouted out things for us to see and do that were within a fifty-mile radius of his home. His rule was that we had to do something educational and then something fun and then something educational and then something fun. My grandmother organized the food, picnic-style, and all the families contributed to the feast.

Here is what happened one year: We started the day at my grandparents' home. Grandpa, with his quirky sense of humor, gave each of the grandchildren a tube of dark red lipstick, much to the dismay of all the mothers—especially when he told us to paint ourselves in designs. Then we went to the local Army base to see the colors raised and hear the commander's speech on why we have Memorial Day. After that, we went to a roller skating rink where even my great-grandmother skated with the help of her big great-grandsons. The rink manager had to get a picture of all four generations of us in roller skates. I'm sure the lipstick decorations helped make us memorable. Then we went to a dairy farm to learn about the dairy industry. I specifically remember my older male cousin picking me up and trying to stuff me into a hay manger as my other cousins laughed. Afterwards, we had a picnic lunch before heading to a copper mine for a tour. We finished the day with swimming and a picnic supper. It was a grand time for all of us cousins to play together and for the adults to talk. Sometimes I would ride with my uncle and cousins as we drove from place to place, and we all sang nonsense songs together. What a precious memory our family had that was made possible by my grandparents who took the time and made the effort to organize it.

Distance can make it harder to maintain relationships, but the effort and other resources it takes are worth it in memories, warmed hearts, and the experience of seeing grandchildren, like Dillon, as their faces light up when they get to see beloved grandparents—even on a computer or telephone screen. The problem is that, if the effort isn't made to maintain those relationships, the expressions on those faces will be restrained, shy, or confused, rather than glad. The children won't have that strong influence of a grandparent who loves them, nor the confidence that comes from knowing that someone loves them dearly unless we make the effort to maintain that relationship—despite the miles in between.

Chapter Eleven

When Your World Crumbles

When I broke my foot during a move, I was irritated and despairing. I didn't have time for that kind of setback, and it hurt. How was I ever going to unpack all the boxes and put things away when I had a broken foot? Of course, my husband was a trooper and tried to take on the whole job himself, but he's not a super hero (although he looks like one and he's my super hero). I was overwhelmed with gratitude when the family pitched in to help. Our daughter and her husband and our son and his wife and the grandchildren and even a nephew all showed up. Our teenage grandsons and the nephew carried heavy boxes and furniture up and down stairs. Our daughters and granddaughters (including steps) helped me put things away. I never would have been able to get everything done by myself. I've often been the one taking care of others, but I was warmed that, when I was hurt, my family saved the day.

We, as the grandparents, are the strong ones—or we were at one time. We are the ones who changed the diapers, made the money to take care of our families, and nursed them back to health when they were sick. We've had experiences that have helped us grow, but as we age, we also have experiences that bring us down. One of the benefits of maintaining strong family relationships is that we can help each other. Even if the roles are reversed and we become the receivers of care, there are often little things we can do for our families and that they can do for us.

For example, when a daughter-in-law became seriously ill, we were able to help pick children up and taxi them to the places they had to be. We were also able to help them by providing meals and other resources. I felt grateful to be able to help and also that they felt able to help me when I broke my foot. It's that kind of give-and-take system that helps families function.

Now that Lily is a grown woman with children of her own, she is in a position to help her grandparents and step-grandparents, who helped her after her parents' divorce and as she was growing up. She has one of her grandfathers living with her. He helped her through tumultuous times when she was a child, and she is happy to help him. In fact, she had to fight to have him stay with her. She said, "My siblings and stepsiblings all love him so much they offered to pay for him to visit them or have him come live with them, but I was the winner and I got him."

Lily is grateful to her grandfather because of what he has done for her. As mentioned in another chapter, she said,

> The grandpa living with me now taught me a love of everything I love now. He gave me the complete works of Shakespeare in sixth grade. Opera. Power of Myth, Joseph Campbell. Crossword puzzles. He's

ornery on the outside, but he's the kindest man ever. He's taught me more about service than anyone. While he lives with us, I never fold laundry, I don't empty the dishwasher or do gardening. He just likes to be useful and serve others. Grandpa is gruff, so it's harder for my children to know him, but my baby is the light of his life.

On the other hand, her relationship with her grandmother is not as positive because of her grandmother's behavior. While Lily acknowledges that her grandmother had a terrible life, so there are reasons for her problems, it's been hard for Lily to come to terms with the issues that impacted Lily herself. She said,

> My grandma and me, we have a weird relationship, but I love her anyway. She's made it tough to learn to live with her and not get my feelings hurt. It does influence how I would treat my children and grandchildren. For example, she plays favorites, and they change, so you're never sure which one you are. I know she loves her children and tries to do things for them, but it's hard accepting her for herself when she does these things. I finally learned to forgive her. I only blew up at her once. I told her I was sorry, and we both cried and said sorry, and it was over. I feel like I'm more mature than she is now. She lies to get attention or because it's easier than telling the truth. So I kind of feel sorry for her. I know why she does it now. It's not that she's spiteful. It's easier to love her now that I know other people like her.

The beautiful point of Lily's story is the forgiveness and saying sorry. That is something she can give to her grandmother and teach her own grandchildren.

Deirdre and Tom have also experienced the role reversals that come with parents aging. Deirdre said,

> The first time I realized my father was not indestructible was when my kids had kids and my father was in his seventies. We all went on a trip to a lake resort where we stayed in a condo, and my father rented wave runners and canoes for us to play with. He took me out on the lake on a wave runner and dumped us both because he lost control when he tried to make the wave runner do a doughnut. I had to save him. I towed him and the wave runner to shore. He was terribly embarrassed to have gotten us in that situation. Later, after my mother died, his health went downhill very quickly. It dropped alarmingly, to the point he could no longer take care of himself. My sister and I had to take turns living with him and caring for him 24/7 for a number of years until he died. If it hadn't been for government subsidized home health care, I don't know what we would have done, because my sister and I both worked. My children and grandchildren occasionally helped care for him and visited him, including my son's second wife and her children, which gave me some relief. Tom, too. He was fantastic about staying with Dad so I could go out some. I just hope that, when we get that old, they remember how we treated my parents.

Caring for grandparents is a common situation. Cathy remembered,

> My father did have me start sleeping over at my grandparents more when my grandfather's Parkinson's got really bad. On the weekends, I would do

his exercises so he didn't become rigid. It was sad because he lost his speech. I saw my grandfather regress to an infant form. I did it because he was my grandfather and I had to, but I didn't like it much. I had to feed him, and he just got to where he had soup. He never complained and never said "poor me," and I admired that. My husband and I moved in with my grandmother when she was ill. We watched her and took care of the house. Then she went to a nursing home. She lived until she was 101. Her body just gave out, but she was pretty sharp. They had her on steroids, and the side effects killed her.

Cathy said that taking care of her grandparents has affected her and how she wants to be treated. She said, "I don't bother anybody when I'm sick. I don't want anyone to have to take care of me. Knock on wood. I'm pretty healthy."

But if something does happen to her, she's set a good example for her children about how to treat grandparents—one she's learned from her grandmother. She said, "My grandmother had the stereotypical evil stepmother. My grandmother and her two sisters were treated really badly, like Cinderella. But the irony of it was that she took in her stepmother and took care of her until she died because her own children wouldn't take her in."

Now that people are living longer, care-giving often becomes multi-generational. Leslie has learned what it is to receive care while being the caregiver. She takes care of her father, who lives a few blocks away, but she has needs herself. She said,

> I have to have chemotherapy because I have cancer, and I have another chemo treatment this week. My son and his wife are coming to stay with me. They are easy to have come over. They are good about doing

> the cooking and things themselves. They say they remember how often we took them in when they were first married and having financial problems. In fact, my son's wife lived with us while he was deployed in Afghanistan. His wife said she's lived longer with me than with my son.

Alyssa also has had to go to great lengths and great distances to help her in-laws. She said, "We've driven to Nebraska three times so far since summer trying to help my husband's grandparents to get ready to move up to Washington to live with their son. When they need help, we try to arrange things to go help. It's not easy since they're so far away."

Mitzi and Dick have had to rely on family for help. Mitzi said, "I had lung cancer for three years, and Dick had open heart surgery, so we had to have help there. We've been lucky, though, that we've never had the grandchildren really sick. But we pull together as a family. Everybody has always prayed for each other and done what they could."

The way families pull together is inspiring. Gloria tells about her neighbor and how she is helping her family. She said,

> One of our neighbors is raising her eight-year-old granddaughter because the girl's parents became addicted to drugs after an automobile accident. The parents are in rehab in Florida, but they've been in rehab forever, and the grandparents are now attempting to get full-time custody. At the same time, they're taking care of the woman's seventy-eight-year-old mother, who this month has been in the hospital three times for serious health problems.

Life can be tough. When life gets tough, we sometimes suffer from the most debilitating illness of all—victimhood. One interviewee said she learned an important lesson from her stepfather. She said, "Many years ago, in a moment of frustration, I vented to my stepfather that life continued to be more challenging. He looked at me as if he were disappointed and said, 'Of course it does.' From that, I learned not to whine."

Our family experienced some of the worst kinds of tragedy—the death of our oldest daughter when she was eighteen, and then the next year the diagnosis of my husband with a terminal disease. Together, we suffered through months and months of time in the hospital in intensive care units. The impact on our family was horrible. The younger children felt cut adrift. Although they knew at some level that we loved them, we could not be there for them when we, as parents, had to be in the hospital. We were lucky enough to have grandparents nearby who could give the children some attention and support us as parents by being there for our children.

I'll always remember the poignant scene that took place while sitting with my husband in my in-laws' living room the morning after our daughter died. We were stunned and heartbroken and unable to function, and my in-laws, seeing a need to step in, fed our remaining children and surrounded us with love. Later, when my husband was in and out of the hospital, my parents sometimes had the children go with them to their cabin. The grandparents supplied the solidarity and normalcy that we badly needed and for which I am grateful. Their willingness to help in a time of need still influences us as we try to help our children and grandchildren now.

Not all helping situations are centered around illness or sadness. Sometimes the care giving can be fun. For example, Christopher recalled taking his ninety-two-year-old stepfather to Hawaii. It has been difficult for their family to realize that Ed and Ann are getting old. Ed did many things with Christopher as he was growing up that he wants his own children to experience. Ann said,

When they were younger, they did the same things with Ed that Christopher did with him. Ed taught Christopher to ski and shoot and garden. We would take trips, and Ed taught him how to cook outdoors and fish. We just had great times. Like I said, when we were younger, we'd take them to our cabin where we had horses. Ed taught them to ride and how to take care of the horses. We showed them how to tube down the river. We showed them how to shoot. We did the same with his children that we did with Christopher. His kids grew up thinking Ed was their actual grandfather. Christopher says, "You need to show my kids what you showed me, like gardening." He doesn't realize how old Ed is now. He can't do the same things that he did when he was younger. And my health is really poor. Now, to keep in touch, we call the kids all the time. We tell them funny stories about when Ed was a boy. They just cuddle up and like us to read to them. We usually just sit and let them tell us their stories, and if they want advice, we give them advice.

The lessons to be learned from the experiences of the people interviewed for this book are centered around the stability and love that come from years of established relationships—relationships that required time and effort and being involved in each others' lives. Another lesson is that these people were willing to put themselves out when help was needed. That's what families should do.

Conclusion

This project has been a great blessing to me. I am encouraged by the many loving families I have interviewed, and I am grateful for the generosity of so many who have been willing to share their lives and their wisdom with me so I could share it with you, my readers.

I reiterate—grandparents really can save the world. I know this because so many grandparents already are saving those close to them. I hope this book encourages grandparents everywhere and gives people ideas and inspiration to improve their relationships with their own families.

Happy grandparenting!

Interviewee Biographies

I interviewed many people, and I'm very grateful to them for sharing their stories with me and you. Of course, they are all distinct personalities in my mind, but they may not be in readers' minds as you try to remember who did what or had what relationships. I was lucky enough to be able to interview many individuals, and some multi-generational families, which means there are some relationships that may be hard to remember. For your benefit, here are some short biographies so you can remember who is who and what their circumstances are. Some people wanted me to use their real names, and some wanted me to use pseudonyms, if there were especially sensitive issues in their families. For reasons of privacy, I will not say which names are real and which ones are made up. However, all of the situations are real. **Alyssa's** grandparents live far from her, as do her husband's. Alyssa and her husband feel good about traveling long distances to help their grandparents.

GRANDPARENTING THE BLENDED FAMILY

Angela and Mitch have two daughters of their own, one of whom is Tiffany, whose husband is Steve. They also took in their daughter's best friend, Brenda, when her family situation was not good. Brenda's children, including her son, Josh, lived with Angela and Mitch after Brenda's marriage ended in divorce. They consider Angela and Mitch to be their real grandparents.

Ann and Ed are Christopher's mother and stepfather.

Ashley is Diane and Randy's daughter. She helped them welcome her nephew, Riley's half-sister, into the family.

Bethany has children, grandchildren, and step-grandchildren because of a second marriage. She and her husband don't live near any of their children, but they maintain relationships through visits, presents, and electronic means.

Caleb became a step-grandfather when he married for the second time and his new stepdaughter became pregnant. He has helped raise his step-grandchildren and considers them his.

Cari is grateful for her grandparents and the way her parents are being wonderful grandparents to her children.

Caroline has several children and grandchildren. She is always looking for ways to help them, although she has limited means.

Cathy has a large family and several children of her own. She took care of her grandfather when he got Parkinson's and also her grandmother. Her grandparents were a major influence in her life.

Christopher's parents divorced when he was a child. His mother, Ann, then married Ed. His father, Dick, then married Mitzi. Christopher has parents, stepparents, grandparents, and step-grandparents, siblings, stepsiblings, and several children of his own—a truly blended family.

Diane and Randy have several daughters and a son, who was divorced, remarried, and then committed suicide. Their son's son is Riley. Riley's mother, Bridget, remarried (to Greg) and had other children, including Emma, who became like a grandchild to Diane and Randy. Their daughter, Ashley, joined with Diane and Randy in welcoming Emma into their family.

Dick and Mitzi are Christopher's father and stepmother.

Ellen was divorced and then remarried. She grew up in an abusive home. Her daughter is married and has a son, Dillon. Her son is married to a woman who already had a daughter, Stephanie, and now has a son, Austin. They live several states away from Ellen, although Dillon lives only a few blocks away.

Gene was in foster care for several years after his grandfather died, because he couldn't get along with his parents. His grandfather was a major influence in his life.

Gloria and her husband live far away from their children, but they are very connected through visits and technology. They have five children, three of whom are Lanie, Laurie, and Joni. They have several grandchildren, including Kristen, Megan, and Jessica.

Julie was adopted when she was five. She appreciates how well she was accepted by her adoptive grandparents and tries to follow their examples in her relationships with her own grandchildren.

Leslie has several children, grandchildren, and a step-grandchild. She tries to include all of them and let them know she loves them, although she has cancer and she doesn't always feel very well.

Lily's father left her and her mother when Lily was a child. Her grandfather and step-grandfather helped to raise her. Lily feels blessed to have several layers of natural, step, and half-siblings, parents, and grandparents.

Melanie is grateful for her grandmother and the example her grandmother set for her, especially considering her tumultuous childhood where Melanie witnessed abuse, the divorce of her parents, her mother's remarriage to someone Melanie did not like, and other hardships.

GRANDPARENTING THE BLENDED FAMILY

Melissa babysits her grandson so her daughter can go to work. The funny things he says delight her.

Myfanwy and Sean have grandparents and step-grandparents, although they do not have children of their own. They have been influenced by their grandparents' examples and especially appreciate the things their grandparents have done for them.

Roslyn and Stephen have a daughter and a son, and both of their children's marriages ended in divorce. Their son's son, is Tim, who lived with them from seventh grade to high school graduation. Their daughter's daughters, who lived with them until they were grown, are Jennie and Charlotte.

Sharon's father left her family when she was a child. Her grandparents were very influential in Sharon's life. Both of Sharon's parents have remarried, giving her and her children several diverse types of relationships.

Shelley's mother died when Shelley's youngest sister was born. Shelley's grandmother moved in with the family and helped raise them for several years. She was a major influence on Shelley's life.

Stan and Dolores have children and grandchildren and step-grandchildren. One daughter was divorced and remarried. Her ex-husband got custody of the children, which made it difficult to maintain relationships with them. Their daughter remarried and brought them new step-grandchildren. Their other daughter went through some hard times, too, and so Stan and Dolores were able to step in and help by taking their grandchildren on trips to their cabin and giving them other opportunities.

Tom and Deirdre have a large family. They have several children, including a son who divorced and remarried, which gave them a new daughter-in-law and new grandchildren.

Tony's new in-laws make life difficult for him and his wife, although he tries to be supportive of them.

About Dene Low

Dene Low is a grandparent. She thought she knew how to grandparent until she interviewed over thirty grandparents for this book, who shared their wisdom and experiences. Dene is a former journalist and is an award-winning author of novels, short stories, articles, and scholarly anthology chapters. She has a Ph.D. and is currently a university professor. When she's not writing, teaching, or playing with her family, she is touring the United States with her husband on their motorcycles.

About Familius

Welcome to a place where mothers are celebrated, not compared. Where heart is at the center of our families, and family at the center of our homes. Where boo boos are still kissed, cake beaters are still licked, and mistakes are still okay. Welcome to a place where books—and family—are beautiful. Familius: a book publisher dedicated to helping families be happy.

Familius was founded in 2012 with the intent to align the founders' love of publishing and family with the digital publishing renaissance which occurred simultaneously with the Great Recession. The founders believe that the traditional family is the basic unit of society, and that a society is only as strong as the families that create it. Familius's mission is to help families be happy. We invite you to participate with us in strengthening your family by being part of the Familius family. Go to www.familius.com to subscribe and receive information about our books, articles, and videos.

Website: www.familius.com
Facebook: www.facebook.com/paterfamilius
Twitter: @familiustalk, @paterfamilius1
Pinterest: www.pinterest.com/familius

CPSIA information can be obtained at www.ICGtesting.com
Printed in the USA
BVOW01s0910101013
333371BV00002B/9/P

Anatomy of a TORNADO

by Terri Dougherty

**Consultant:
Dr. Jon Ahlquist
Department of Earth, Ocean, and Atmospheric Science
Florida State University**

LOMBARDO

CAPSTONE PRESS
a capstone imprint

Velocity is published by Capstone Press,
1710 Roe Crest Drive, North Mankato, Minnesota 56003.
www.capstonepub.com

Copyright © 2011 by Capstone Press, a Capstone imprint.
All rights reserved. No part of this publication may be reproduced in whole or in part, or stored in a retrieval system, or transmitted in any form or by any means, electronic, mechanical, photocopying, recording, or otherwise, without written permission of the publisher. For information regarding permission, write to Capstone Press, 1710 Roe Crest Drive, North Mankato, Minnesota 56003.

Library of Congress Cataloging-in-Publication Data
Dougherty, Terri.
Anatomy of a tornado / by Terri Dougherty.
p. cm.—(Velocity. Disasters)
Summary: "Describes tornadoes, including their causes, prediction, and effects"—Provided by publisher.
Includes bibliographical references and index.
ISBN 978-1-4296-5494-4 (library binding)
ISBN 978-1-4296-6281-9 (paperback)
1. Tornadoes—Juvenile literature. I. Title. II. Series.
QC955.2.D68 2011
551.55'3—dc22   2010027649

Editorial Credits
Carrie Braulick Sheely, editor; Alison Thiele, designer; Wanda Winch, media researcher; Laura Manthe, production specialist

Photo Credits
Capstone Studio: Karon Dubke, 8, 13 (clock), 30 (egg), 31 (toilet paper), 40-43 (all); Corbis: Bettmann, 33, Eric Nguyen, 12 (right), Jim Reed Photography/Jim Reed, 22-23; Dreamstime/Dan Van Den Broeke, 20 (top); FEMA News Photo: Andrea Booher, 34-35, Bob McMillan, 44, Greg Henshall, 39 (top), Lara Shane, 45; ©1994 Gene E. Moore, 13 (top), ©2008 Gene E. Moore, 10 (bottom right), 11 (top right, bottom right); Getty Images Inc., 16 (right), National Archives/National Center for Atmospheric Research/Time Life Pictures, 20 (middle), NOAA, 20 (bottom); Minnesota Historical Society: Minneapolis Star, 31 (top); NOAA: NWS, 18, NWS Office, Wilmington, Ohio/Fred Stewart, 38-39, NWS/John Jarboe, 28-29, NWS/SPC, 19; Nova Development Corporation, 13 (calendar); Photo courtesy of Sharon Watson, the Kansas Adjutant General's Department, Topeka, Kansas, 26-27; photolibrary: Peter Arnold/Weatherstock, 12 (left); Shutterstock: AridOcean, 13 (map), Armin rose, 21 (top), jam4travel, cover (house), 5, mart, 16 (map), Niels van Gijn, 17 (top), Oculo, mosaic square design element, Nikonov, metal background, Photography Perspectives-Jeff Smith, 4, Sebastian Kaulitzki, scratched metal texture, Stanislav E. Petrov, cement wall, Vasyl Helevachuk, 30 (right); Steve Molenaar, 10-11 (back); Tim Samaras, 21 (bottom); TornadoVideos.net, 24-25; University of Chicago, 27 (bottom), Wikipedia: Justin Hobson, cover (tornado), 16 (left)

Printed in the United States of America in North Mankato, Minnesota.
050215   008958R

TABLE OF CONTENTS

Introduction: Sudden Impact!   4

Chapter 1: Tornado Basics   6

Chapter 2: Predicting and Studying a Tornado   18

Chapter 3: Sizing up a Tornado   26

Chapter 4: Record Breakers   32

Chapter 5: Tornado Safety   40

     Glossary   46
     Read More   47
     Internet Sites   47
     Index   48

Introduction

Sudden Impact!

Families huddled in basements as a whirling tornado headed their way. First came the sound of a freight train. Then the sound of shattering glass. With a roar and a whoosh, the twirling wind tore at everything in its way.

After just a few minutes, it was all over. But the tornado that hit Parkersburg, Iowa, in May 2008 left behind a path of destruction. The powerful tornado ripped apart nearly half the town. Homes and businesses became piles of rubble. Cars were smashed by falling trees, and the ground was littered with splintered wood. Seven people were killed.

A tornado is a column of rapidly spinning air. It reaches from a storm cloud to the ground. Cars, houses, and almost anything else in a tornado's path can be completely destroyed.

The strongest winds in the world are found in a tornado. Ground-level tornado wind speeds can't be measured with current technology. Instead, a tornado's wind speed is estimated based on the amount of damage it causes. The most powerful tornadoes have wind speed estimates of more than 200 miles (320 kilometers) per hour.

Weather instruments can sometimes record tornado wind speeds above ground level. The strongest tornado wind speed ever recorded was 318 miles (512 km) per hour. This tornado struck near Moore, Oklahoma, on May 3, 1999.

About 1,000 tornadoes strike the United States each year. Most hit during "tornado season," which is from March through July. Tornadoes are more common in the southern United States in early spring. In northern states, more occur in late spring and early summer.

FACT: Tornadoes are sometimes called twisters.

Chapter 1

TORNADO BASICS

Thunderstorms

The sky turns dark in the distance. You hear the low rumble of thunder. These signs tell you a thunderstorm could be headed your way.

Thunderstorms bring thunder, lightning, and rain. Heavy downpours, strong winds, and **hail** are also possible. And a few thunderstorms bring something else—tornadoes.

How does a thunderstorm lead to the formation of a tornado? First, it's important to know how thunderstorms develop.

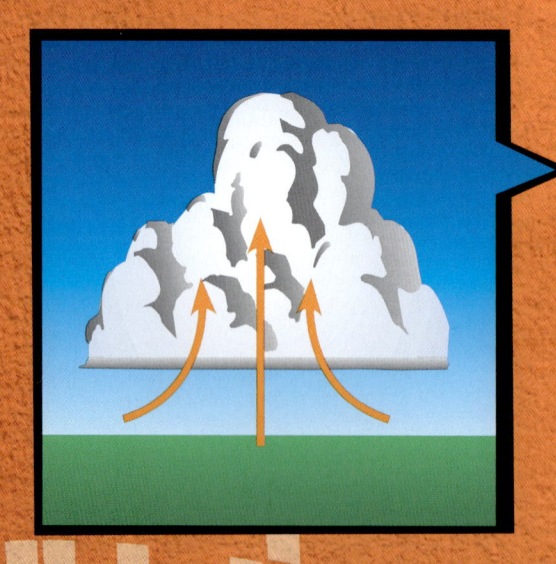

1. Thunderstorms form when warm, moist air rises. An updraft of wind pushes the warm air higher into the sky. The water vapor in the air cools and **condenses**, forming water droplets and a cloud. As more heat rises, a towering cumulonimbus cloud forms.

hail—balls of ice that fall during some thunderstorms; hail forms when water droplets become coated with icy layers as winds blow the droplets up and down
condense— to change from a gas into a liquid

2. As water droplets and ice in the cloud grow, the updraft can no longer hold them. They fall as rain or hail, dragging down the air around them. This sinking air is a downdraft. The downdraft is made of cooler air than the updraft. As the storm grows, more updrafts and downdrafts may form.

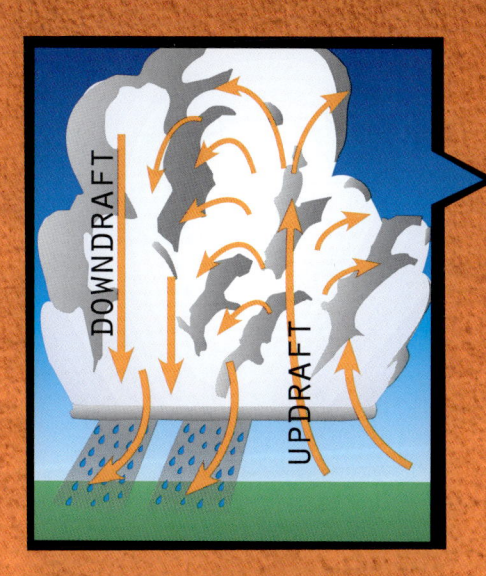

3. A thunderstorm usually dies after about 30 minutes. By this time, the rain and the downdraft have usually cooled the air around the storm. Then there is no more warm air feeding the storm with moisture.

LIGHTNING AND THUNDER

A storm cloud creates lightning because the ice and water droplets in the cloud have electrical charges. The positive and negative charges build up. The electricity discharges in a bolt of lightning. The bolt then heats the air around it. The air heats and expands so rapidly that it explodes in a bang that we call thunder.

FACT! Tornadoes can form at any time of day. But they usually occur in the afternoon or evening.

7

Supercells

The storms most often responsible for causing tornadoes aren't just ordinary storms. These monster storms are named for their size and force—they're called supercells.

The strong wind at the top of the supercell creates a spinning column of air underneath it. An updraft of air then lifts the middle of the column, bringing it upright. This twirling column of air is called a mesocyclone. It is usually 2 to 10 miles (3.2 to 16 km) wide. It can reach 50,000 feet (15,240 meters) into the sky. In about three of every 10 supercells, the mesocyclone forms a tornado.

MOVING QUICKLY

The wind high in a supercell also helps keep the storm going. High-level wind blows faster than the wind below it. Because of this, the supercell leans forward. As the storm leans, the downdraft is pulled away from the updraft.

MOVING SLOWLY

THE SPINNING MESOCYCLONE

To get an idea of how the mesocyclone rotates, hold a roll of paper towels horizontally. Put one hand on top of the roll and the other hand below it. Push forward with your top hand. The tube rotates. Your top hand is like the strong upper-level wind making the air below it spin.

Now use your bottom hand to push the tube upright. Your bottom hand is like the updraft of air. Your spinning mesocyclone is now in a position to become a tornado.

Spreading air forms the cloud's anvil.

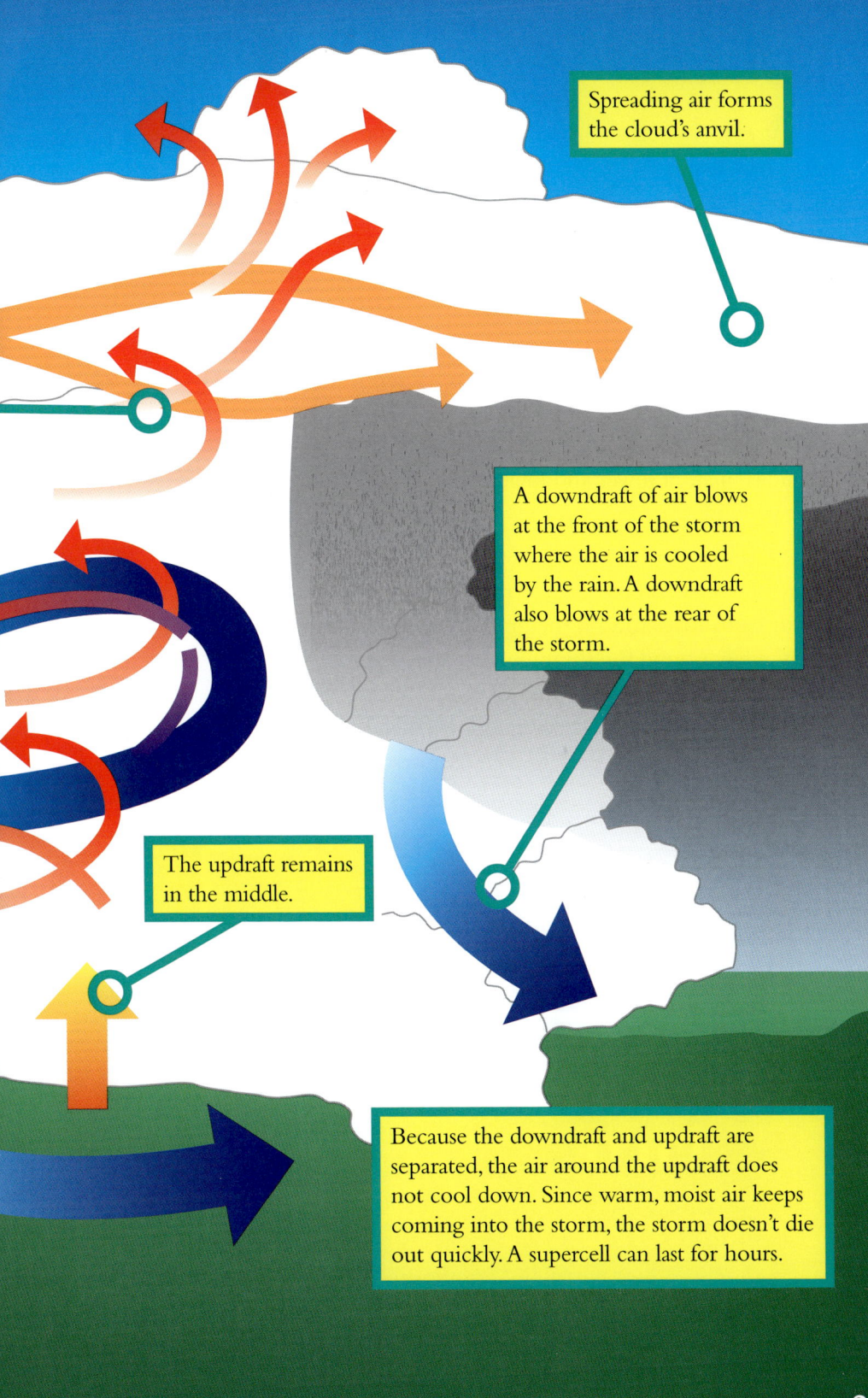

A downdraft of air blows at the front of the storm where the air is cooled by the rain. A downdraft also blows at the rear of the storm.

The updraft remains in the middle.

Because the downdraft and updraft are separated, the air around the updraft does not cool down. Since warm, moist air keeps coming into the storm, the storm doesn't die out quickly. A supercell can last for hours.

Tornado!

If a spinning mesocyclone starts reaching toward the ground, it is called a funnel cloud. And if the funnel cloud reaches the ground, its name changes to a tornado.

Scientists have several ideas about why tornadoes form:

One idea is that the mesocyclone may move downward when the winds beneath it are weak. The column of air is like a pipe, and air can only get into it from the bottom. The slowly moving air below the mesocyclone is drawn upward and starts to spin. The spinning column then grows longer. It pulls in air at lower and lower levels until it touches the ground.

A sinking current of air at the back of the storm also may play a role in tornado formation. This downdraft of dry air moves toward the ground. As it moves, it may wrap around the spinning mesocyclone and pull it down. The rotating column of air stretches and gets thinner. It spins faster, just like a figure skater spins faster when pulling in her arms. Finally, the mesocyclone reaches the ground.

FACT: Scientists think the rear downdraft might get sucked up into the mesocyclone near the ground. This occurrence could give a tornado more power.

TORNADO LIFE CYCLE

1. FUNNEL CLOUD STAGE: The funnel cloud reaches down from the thunderstorm.

2. **Mature stage:**

The funnel cloud reaches the ground and becomes a tornado. The tornado may grow wider and change color. Toward the end of its life, a tornado becomes narrower. It may look like a rope or form loops. The tornado remains very powerful, though. Its energy is centralized into a small area.

3. **Dissipating stage:**

The tornado continues getting narrower before disappearing. It may appear to break into pieces.

One Name, Many Looks

All tornadoes are spinning columns of air, but not every tornado looks the same.

Color

A tornado's color is affected by the dirt and **debris** it pulls up from the ground. The dirt and debris can make a tornado look red or black.

Sunlight also affects a tornado's color. If sunlight shines on the front of a tornado, the tornado looks white. The tornado looks black or dark gray if sunlight is behind it. If the sun is setting, the tornado may look red or gold.

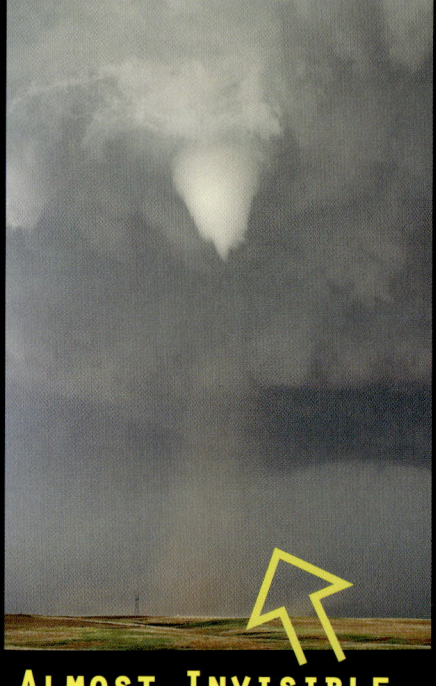

Almost Invisible

Sometimes a tornado's walls cannot be seen. In these cases, the air is too dry for the water vapor to condense. A dust cloud on the ground and a rotating cloud above it are the only clues to the tornado's presence.

Suction Vortices

A tornado may contain more than one twisting column of air. These tornadoes are called multiple vortex tornadoes. The smaller swirls of air are called suction vortices. Scientists think most tornadoes have suction vortices, but that they often aren't visible.

debris—the remains of something that has been destroyed

12

Shape Shifters

Tornadoes can take on one of several shapes. A tornado is often shaped like a funnel. But it could look like a large wedge or a thin rope. A large wedge-shaped tornado can be more than 1 mile (1.6 km) wide.

Q: According to statistics, what's the most likely time and place for a tornado to hit?

A: Place = Center of Oklahoma

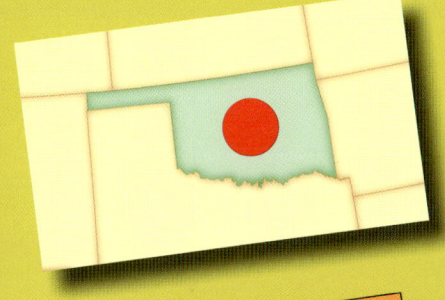

Time = 5:00 P.M.

First 2 weeks in MAY

Tornado Alley

More tornadoes strike the United States than any other country in the world. Most U.S. tornadoes strike the central part of the country. Tornadoes are common in this area because the land is flat. There are no mountains to stop warm, moist air from the Gulf of Mexico from moving north. It meets cooler, dry air coming from Canada. The meeting of cool air and warm air makes thunderstorms more likely to develop.

So many tornadoes occur in the center of the United States that the area earned the name "Tornado Alley." Tornadoes usually strike Tornado Alley in spring, with strong tornadoes peaking in May.

An area stretching from Texas to Georgia is called "Dixie Alley" or "Southern Tornado Alley." Tornadoes often strike this area in winter and spring, with strong tornadoes peaking in April. Thunderstorms, tropical storms, or hurricanes can bring tornadoes to the area.

Numbers represent the average annual number of tornadoes to hit each state. Statistics recorded from 1953-2004.

45 Nebraska

22 Colorado

FACT: Tornadoes have occurred in every state in the United States and on every continent except Antarctica.

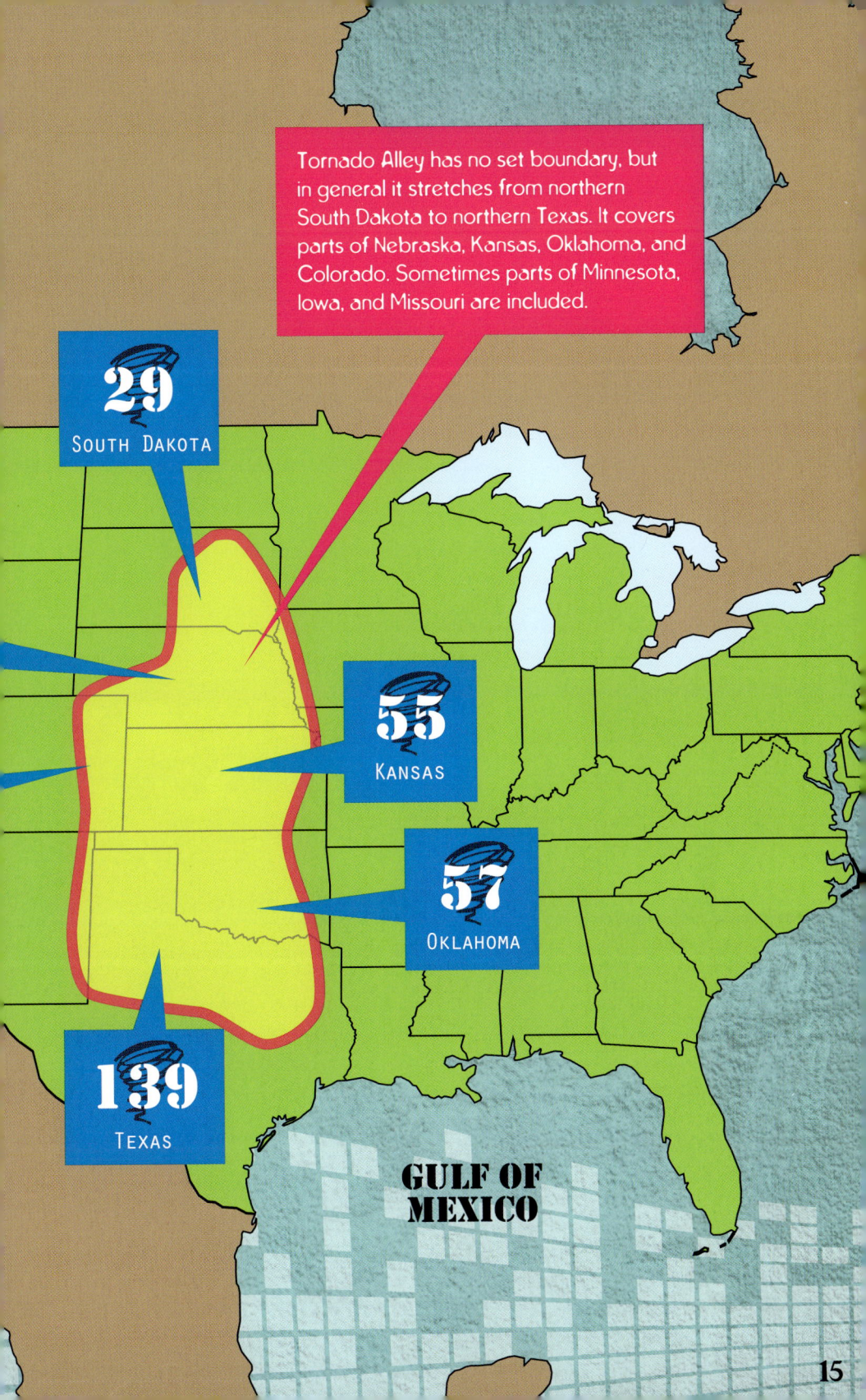

Tornado Alley has no set boundary, but in general it stretches from northern South Dakota to northern Texas. It covers parts of Nebraska, Kansas, Oklahoma, and Colorado. Sometimes parts of Minnesota, Iowa, and Missouri are included.

29 South Dakota

55 Kansas

57 Oklahoma

139 Texas

GULF OF MEXICO

Tornadoes around the World

Even though more tornadoes occur in the United States than anywhere else, other countries are also likely to have tornadoes.

tornado in Manitoba

CANADA: In Canada about 100 tornadoes are reported each year. Besides the United States, Canada gets more tornadoes than any other country. Most occur in the southcentral portion of the country. Tornado season in Canada extends from April to September.

GREAT BRITAIN: About 30 tornadoes hit Great Britain each year. In 1981, 105 were reported on one day, although they caused little damage.

ARGENTINA: A few violent tornadoes form in Argentina each year. On January 10, 1973, a strong tornado struck the town of San Justo. It killed more than 50 people and damaged hundreds of homes.

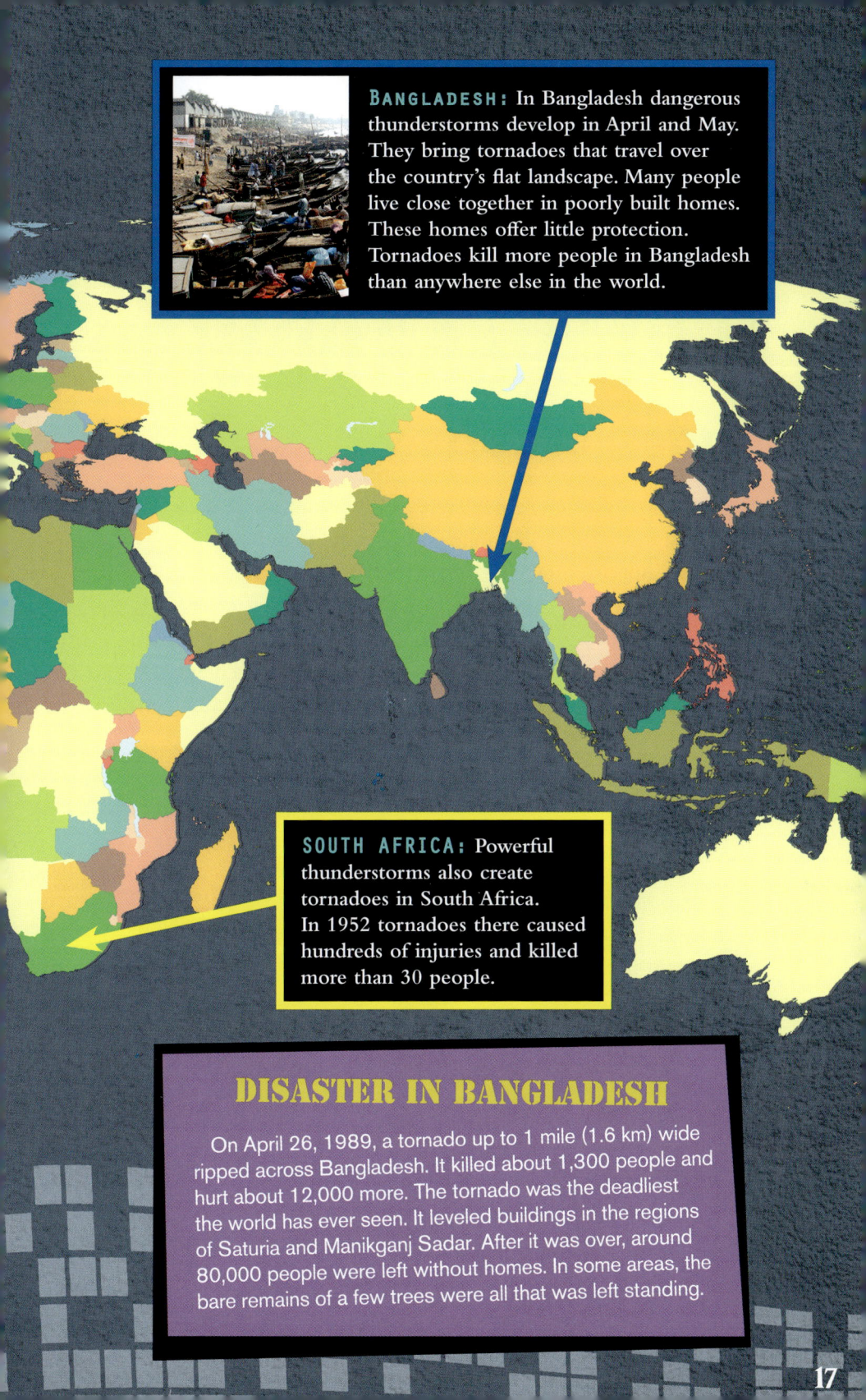

BANGLADESH: In Bangladesh dangerous thunderstorms develop in April and May. They bring tornadoes that travel over the country's flat landscape. Many people live close together in poorly built homes. These homes offer little protection. Tornadoes kill more people in Bangladesh than anywhere else in the world.

SOUTH AFRICA: Powerful thunderstorms also create tornadoes in South Africa. In 1952 tornadoes there caused hundreds of injuries and killed more than 30 people.

DISASTER IN BANGLADESH

On April 26, 1989, a tornado up to 1 mile (1.6 km) wide ripped across Bangladesh. It killed about 1,300 people and hurt about 12,000 more. The tornado was the deadliest the world has ever seen. It leveled buildings in the regions of Saturia and Manikganj Sadar. After it was over, around 80,000 people were left without homes. In some areas, the bare remains of a few trees were all that was left standing.

Chapter 2

Predicting and Studying a Tornado

Tornado Forecasts

National and local weather forecasters closely monitor weather conditions. They then warn the public when severe thunderstorms and tornadoes are approaching. The National Weather Service (NWS) Storm Prediction Center in Norman, Oklahoma, watches for severe weather in all states except Alaska and Hawaii. Forecasters at the center look for conditions that may create a tornado. They issue forecasts each day that tell where severe weather may occur.

NWS weather forecasters at work

Tornado Watches

If tornadoes are likely to develop in an area, the Storm Prediction Center issues a **tornado watch**. The watch alerts local NWS offices, the public, and workers in the airplane industry. Watches usually last four to six hours.

Tornado Warnings

Most states have one or more local NWS offices. These offices monitor weather conditions close to home. If necessary, the local office issues a **tornado warning**. When the threat has ended, the warning or watch is canceled.

Severe Weather Risk Levels

The Storm Prediction Center issues outlooks that show the risk of severe storm development. It lists the risk as slight, moderate, or high for different areas.

Slight: Well-organized severe thunderstorms are expected. The storms are likely to cover a small area or be few in number. There is a small chance of a large severe storm forming.

Moderate: There is a greater likelihood that several severe thunderstorms will occur in the area.

High: Severe weather is expected to hit a wide area. There is also a greater chance of "extreme severe" weather. This type of weather includes violent tornadoes or very damaging winds that occur across a large area.

---

tornado watch—a message issued by the National Weather Service when conditions are right for a tornado to occur in an area

tornado warning—a message issued by a local National Weather Service office when a tornado has been spotted by onlookers or by radar

19

Forecast Tools

Weather forecasters use a number of tools to help them make accurate predictions.

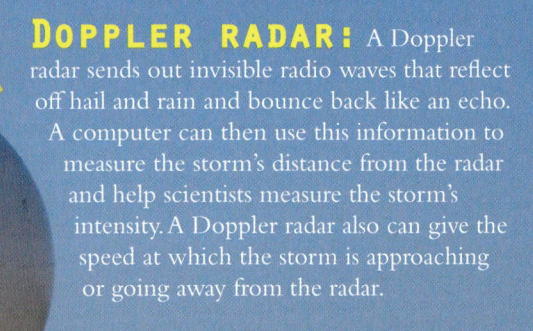

DOPPLER RADAR: A Doppler radar sends out invisible radio waves that reflect off hail and rain and bounce back like an echo. A computer can then use this information to measure the storm's distance from the radar and help scientists measure the storm's intensity. A Doppler radar also can give the speed at which the storm is approaching or going away from the radar.

COMPUTER MODELS: Computer models are complex computer programs that calculate how fast the wind will blow and how much rain will fall. Color graphics then make these forecasts come alive as weather maps that show how the weather is likely to change over time.

SATELLITE IMAGES: Satellites take high-level pictures of clouds. The pictures help forecasters locate areas of moist and dry air.

Weather balloons:

The NWS sends more than 90 weather balloons into the air twice each day. These balloons carry equipment to measure air temperature, air pressure, and humidity levels at different heights.

Air pressure measures the weight of the air above the level at which the measurement is taken. Knowing the air pressure is important because thunderstorms can form when masses of low- and high-pressure air meet.

Thunderstorms also need moisture. Humidity levels tell how much moisture is in the air.

One Tough Tool

Turtles are the toughest tornado tools in a scientist's toolbox. They are designed to survive getting hit by a tornado.

A turtle contains equipment that measures air temperature, air pressure, and humidity levels at ground level. It is placed on the ground in the path of a tornado. To decide where to place turtles, scientists guess which way the tornado will move. They drop off the turtle in the area they feel is likely to get hit. One turtle measured a very sudden drop in air pressure as a tornado passed over it in 2003.

satellite—a machine that circles Earth; satellites send and receive signals from Earth

Spotters and Chasers

Rain and hail pelt the ground. Wind whips through the trees. Storm spotters and chasers are ready for action. They scan the clouds, watching for a funnel cloud to drop from the sky.

Spotters

Storm spotters are trained by the NWS to gather information about severe weather near their homes. The spotters then report storm information to the NWS.

REPORTED INFORMATION INCLUDES:
- FUNNEL CLOUDS
- TORNADOES
- THE DIRECTION A STORM IS MOVING
- ESTIMATED WIND SPEED
- LARGE HAIL

storm chasers near a tornado in Kansas

Chasers

While storm spotters wait for storms to come to them, storm chasers travel to storms. Some chasers are scientists gathering weather data. Other chasers are photographers or videographers. News reporters may also chase a storm to gather information for a story.

Storm chasing can be very dangerous. Chasers risk being killed by the tornado they are chasing. Chasers can be pelted by hail or hurt by flying debris. Some chasers follow unsafe practices. They drive many hours with little sleep. They watch the storm when they should be watching the road. This behavior makes storm chasing even more dangerous.

Storm-Chasing Vehicles

Specially-designed armored vehicles help chasers get close to a storm. The Dominator is one of the most advanced storm chasing vehicles. It is used by scientists on the Discovery Channel's *Storm Chasers* TV show.

A small instrument mast is mounted on the roof. It measures wind speed, air temperature, humidity levels, and other data.

An armored shell covers the Dominator. It is made of sheet metal and Lexan, a strong plastic.

TAKING A CLOSER LOOK

Chasers on the *Storm Chasers* TV show can launch a small remote-control airplane when they are near a tornado. The plane then flies around the tornado. It takes video and releases probes. The probes record video and gather information on temperature, air pressure, and humidity levels.

A high-definition (HD) camera on the roof takes images of storms. It is protected by a strong plastic covering.

Inside the vehicle, a roll cage protects passengers in case the vehicle flips over. The vehicle also has race-car seat belts that securely strap in passengers.

All-terrain tires allow the Dominator to travel on rough roads.

The higher off the ground a vehicle is, the easier it is for high winds to tip it over. The Dominator's frame can drop to the ground to help keep the vehicle stable in high winds. The frame is lowered by flipping a switch in the cockpit.

Chapter 3

SIZING UP A TORNADO

Tornado Rankings

Experts from the NWS estimate a tornado's wind speed by looking at the amount of damage it does. They consider damage to buildings, trees, power line poles, and other structures. NWS workers then use this information to give the tornado a strength ranking on the Enhanced Fujita (EF) Scale. They rank the tornado from 0 to 5 on the scale. The more destructive the tornado, the higher the number. Most tornadoes are rated EF1 in strength.

For an EF5 tornado ranking, damage often includes complete destruction of homes that had solid foundations.

EF SCALE

EF number	3-second wind gust estimate (mph)
0	65-85
1	86-110
2	111-135
3	136-165
4	166-200
5	more than 200

TED FUJITA AND THE F SCALE

Dr. Tetsuya Theodore "Ted" Fujita made the Fujita (F) Scale in 1971. It was the first scale to measure tornado strength. Like scientists using the EF Scale, Fujita studied the damage done by tornadoes. He flew over areas hit by tornadoes to see the damage to homes, trees, cars, and fields. The scale used general terms, such as "well-constructed houses leveled."

In 2007 the EF Scale replaced the F Scale. The new scale describes in detail the degree of damage done to structures. For example, if damage to a large mall were being studied, scientists would consider whether skylights were broken.

Path of Destruction

Tornadoes usually move from southwest to northeast. A typical tornado is about 150 feet (45 m) wide and stays on the ground for about a mile. But a tornado can be much wider and carve out a longer path. A tornado that hit Arkansas on February 5, 2008, destroyed hundreds of homes and killed 12 people. It left a path of damage 123 miles (198 km) long.

Tornadoes often take unpredictable paths. The strong winds of the downdraft can make a tornado quickly move from side to side.

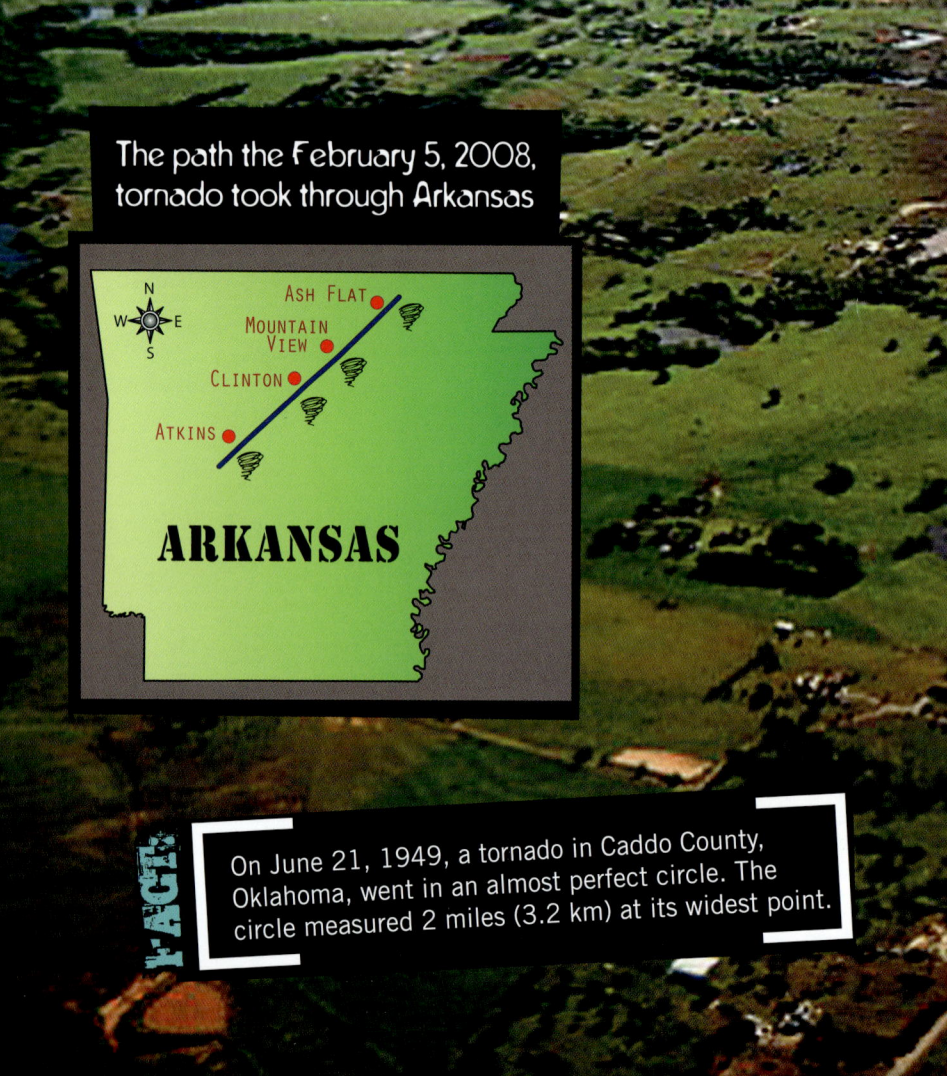

The path the February 5, 2008, tornado took through Arkansas

ASH FLAT
MOUNTAIN VIEW
CLINTON
ATKINS

ARKANSAS

FACT: On June 21, 1949, a tornado in Caddo County, Oklahoma, went in an almost perfect circle. The circle measured 2 miles (3.2 km) at its widest point.

28

Do you see the path of the tornado that went through Oklahoma on May 3, 1999?

Hint: The tornado stripped away grass, trees, and brush to reveal the red clay soil underneath.

The damage a tornado leaves behind often doesn't clearly represent the tornado's path. The damage can seem random. One home may be crushed, while a house next door has only minor damage. This may happen because the tornado was very small but powerful. It may also occur because of suction vortices. A vortex might be small enough to damage one home but miss another.

Tornado Oddities

A tornado's powerful winds make some strange things happen. Amazing tornado tales have been told for hundreds of years. Some of them sound almost too strange to be true. But true or false, the reports keep pouring in.

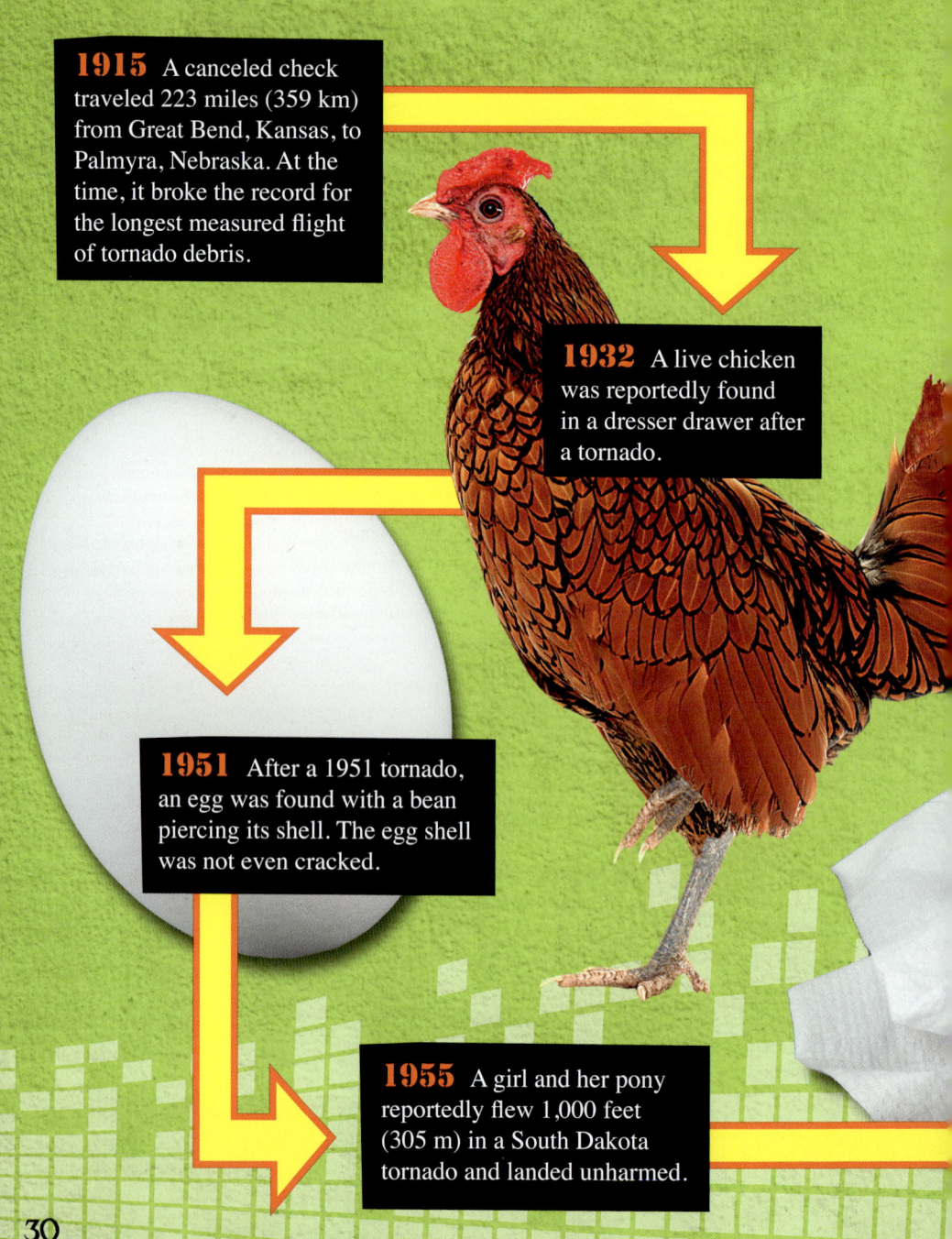

1915 A canceled check traveled 223 miles (359 km) from Great Bend, Kansas, to Palmyra, Nebraska. At the time, it broke the record for the longest measured flight of tornado debris.

1932 A live chicken was reportedly found in a dresser drawer after a tornado.

1951 After a 1951 tornado, an egg was found with a bean piercing its shell. The egg shell was not even cracked.

1955 A girl and her pony reportedly flew 1,000 feet (305 m) in a South Dakota tornado and landed unharmed.

FLYING FEATHERS

After a tornado hits farms, chickens sometimes are found without feathers. This fact has caused some people to think that a tornado's high winds make a chicken's feathers fly off. Some people have suggested that the low pressure of a tornado causes the strange occurrence.

In 1842 Elias Loomis tried to find out how fast winds needed to travel to knock the feathers off a chicken. He put a dead chicken into a cannon and shot the bird out. He reported that the chicken's feathers came out cleanly. Loomis estimated that the chicken flew out at 341 miles (549 km) per hour.

Today's scientists do not blame a tornado's low pressure or high winds for causing bald chickens. A frightened chicken drops out its feathers, or molts. Scientists think a tornado frightens a chicken and then blows away the molted feathers.

dead chicken found after 1939 Minnesota tornado

2006 A 19-year-old man set a record for being thrown by a tornado. The winds pulled him out of his mobile home and dropped him 1,300 feet (396 m) away.

2008 A Minnesota man reported that a tornado unwound a roll of toilet paper in his bathroom and then rewound it in the sink. He also said that although his home's roof was lifted away, his cat's food was still in its bowl.

31

Chapter 4

RECORD BREAKERS

The Deadliest

The Tri-state tornado that cut a path across Missouri, Illinois, and Indiana on March 18, 1925, is the deadliest in U.S. history. The tornado took an estimated 695 lives. Many more people were injured or left without homes.

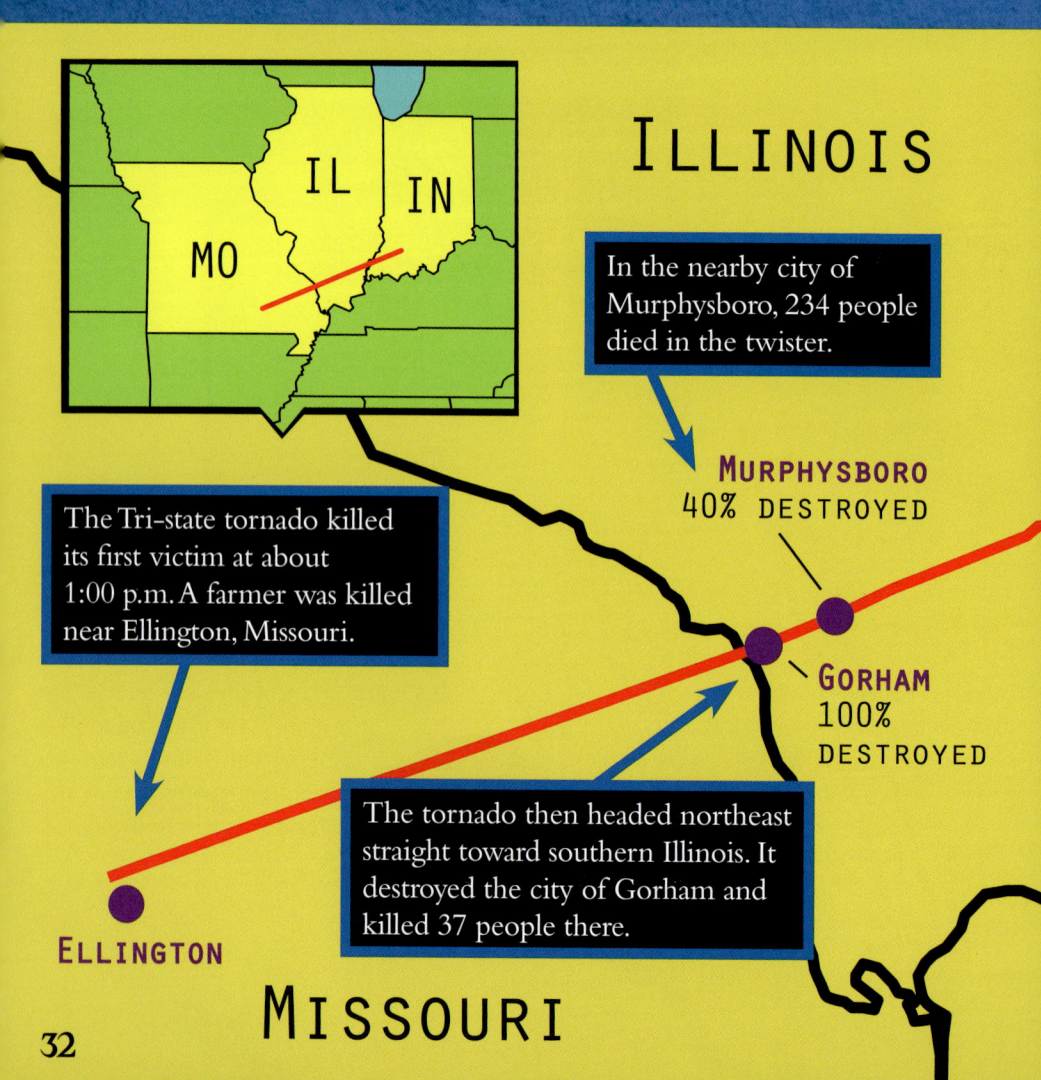

In the nearby city of Murphysboro, 234 people died in the twister.

MURPHYSBORO
40% DESTROYED

The Tri-state tornado killed its first victim at about 1:00 p.m. A farmer was killed near Ellington, Missouri.

GORHAM
100% DESTROYED

The tornado then headed northeast straight toward southern Illinois. It destroyed the city of Gorham and killed 37 people there.

ELLINGTON

ILLINOIS

MISSOURI

32

DEADLIEST U.S. TORNADOES

Date	Place	Deaths**
1. March 18, 1925	Missouri, Illinois, Indiana	695
2. May 6, 1840	Natchez, Missouri	317
3. May 27, 1896	St. Louis, Missouri	255
4. April 5, 1936	Tupelo, Mississippi	216
5. April 6, 1936	Gainesville, Georgia	203

**Death tolls are approximate.

INDIANA

85 FARMS TOTALLY DESTROYED

GRIFFIN 100% DESTROYED

The tornado destroyed a portion of Princeton, Indiana. It then broke up northeast of the town. The killer tornado had traveled 219 miles (352 km).

The tornado ripped across Illinois, claiming more than 600 lives in the state. The tornado then entered Indiana. It destroyed the town of Griffin by ripping apart about 150 homes.

KENTUCKY

The Costliest

Police officer Jody Suit knew the Oklahoma City area well. But she got lost when driving around after a tornado hit on May 3, 1999. All the familiar landmarks had been ripped away by the unforgiving wind. Neighborhoods were flattened, cars became twisted pieces of metal, and power wires hung limply.

FACT: Florida, North Carolina, Georgia, and Alabama have had the most costly severe weather events since 1980. These weather events include hurricanes, droughts, blizzards, tornadoes, and other disasters.

As it rips across the land, a tornado takes a costly toll on the landscape. The tornado that hit the Oklahoma City area in 1999 did more than $1 billion in damage. Moore, Oklahoma, was hit especially hard. Almost half of the city's homes were damaged or destroyed. In Oklahoma City, almost 2,000 houses were beyond repair.

COSTLIEST U.S. TORNADOES

Date	Place	Cost**
1. May 3, 1999	Oklahoma City, Oklahoma	$1 billion
2. May 8, 2003	Oklahoma City, Oklahoma	$370 million
3. June 3, 1980	Grand Island, Nebraska	$285 million
4. April 10, 1979	Wichita Falls, Texas	$278 million
5. May 6, 1975	Omaha, Nebraska	$251 million

**Costs are approximate.

The Worst Outbreaks

On April 3, 1974, Russell Conger was working at the NWS office in Louisville, Kentucky. He saw low clouds come together nearby. Soon the wind got stronger. Rocks flew and hail pounded the windows. He and other NWS employees took cover as a tornado hit the city. In the next 21 minutes, the tornado would damage more than 900 homes beyond repair in Louisville. Yet it was just one of many damaging tornadoes to hit the area that day.

When several tornadoes form over a region, it is called a tornado outbreak. So many tornadoes happened on April 3 and 4, 1974, that it was called a super outbreak.

This super outbreak was one of the worst U.S. tornado outbreaks. The storm lasted for 16 hours and moved across 13 states. It left more than 300 people dead and more than 5,000 injured.

MAJOR TORNADO OUTBREAKS

FEB. 19, 1884

LOCATION HIT: Alabama, Georgia, Illinois, Indiana, Kentucky, Mississippi, North Carolina, South Carolina, Tennessee, Virginia

NUMBER OF TORNADOES: 60

NUMBER OF DEATHS: up to 1,200

APR. 11-12, 1965

LOCATION HIT: Iowa, Illinois, Wisconsin, Indiana, Michigan, Ohio

NUMBER OF TORNADOES: 51

NUMBER OF DEATHS: 260

APR. 3-4, 1974

LOCATION HIT: Alabama, Georgia, Illinois, Indiana, Kentucky, Michigan, Mississippi, North Carolina, Ohio, South Carolina, Tennessee, Virginia, West Virginia

NUMBER OF TORNADOES: 148

NUMBER OF DEATHS: 315

MAY 3, 1999

LOCATION HIT: Oklahoma, Kansas

NUMBER OF TORNADOES: 70

NUMBER OF DEATHS: 55

F5 Tornadoes of Super Outbreak, April 3-4, 1974

= States affected by Super Outbreak

= F5 Tornadoes

= Cities

37

The Strongest

EF5 tornadoes, called F5 tornadoes before 2007, are the most powerful tornadoes. Since 1950 more than 50 of these have left paths of destruction in the United States. These tornadoes have estimated wind speeds that top 200 miles (322 km) per hour.

On April 3, 1974, an F5 tornado roared through Xenia, Ohio, during the super outbreak. Half the city's buildings were damaged.

RECENT U.S. EF5 TORNADOES

Date	Location
May 25, 2008	Parkersburg, Iowa
May 4, 2007	Greensburg, Kansas
May 3, 1999	Bridge Creek/Moore, Oklahoma
April 16, 1998	Waynesboro, Tennessee
April 8, 1998	Pleasant Grove, Alabama
May 27, 1997	Jarrell, Texas
July 18, 1996	Oakfield, Wisconsin
June 16, 1992	Chandler, Minnesota
April 26, 1991	Andover, Kansas
August 28, 1990	Plainfield, Illinois

FACT: The most powerful tornadoes are not always the widest. A narrow rope tornado may be ranked as an EF5.

Chapter 5

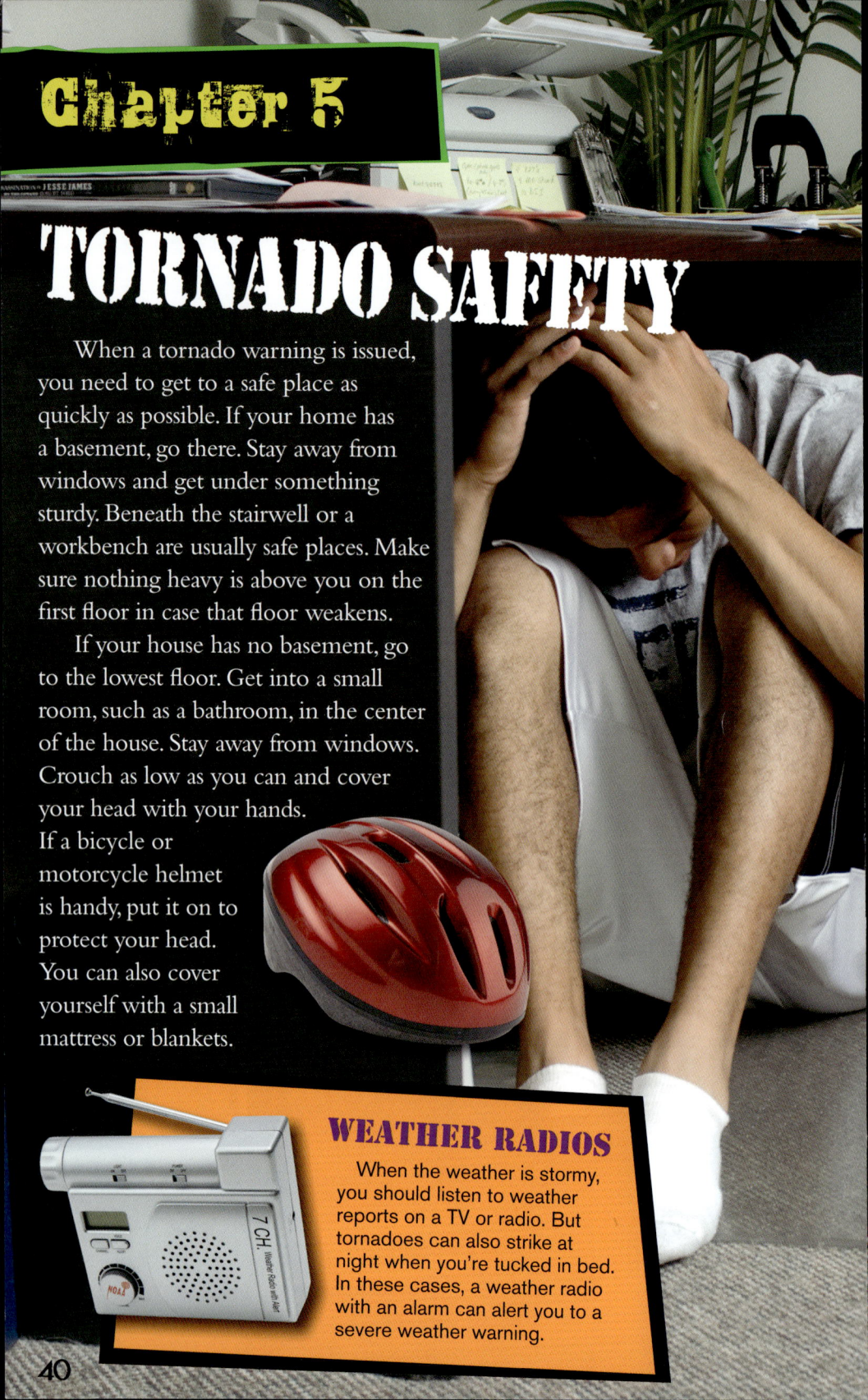

TORNADO SAFETY

When a tornado warning is issued, you need to get to a safe place as quickly as possible. If your home has a basement, go there. Stay away from windows and get under something sturdy. Beneath the stairwell or a workbench are usually safe places. Make sure nothing heavy is above you on the first floor in case that floor weakens.

If your house has no basement, go to the lowest floor. Get into a small room, such as a bathroom, in the center of the house. Stay away from windows. Crouch as low as you can and cover your head with your hands. If a bicycle or motorcycle helmet is handy, put it on to protect your head. You can also cover yourself with a small mattress or blankets.

WEATHER RADIOS

When the weather is stormy, you should listen to weather reports on a TV or radio. But tornadoes can also strike at night when you're tucked in bed. In these cases, a weather radio with an alarm can alert you to a severe weather warning.

Never stay in a mobile home in a tornado warning. A mobile home is less sturdy than a home with a basement. A tornado can easily destroy a mobile home, even if it is tied down. Leave the mobile home and quickly go to a tornado shelter. A sturdy building nearby also may offer protection.

tornado shelter

If you have nowhere else to go, lie facedown in a ditch or on low ground. Stay as far away as you can from trees and cars. Cover your head with your hands.

FACT: Many schools have tornado drills. If your school doesn't, be sure you know a safe place to go in your school. The basement is a good place. A hallway in the middle of the school on the lowest floor might also work. Always stay away from windows.

41

Tornado Myths

For years, people have passed along stories about how to stay safe during a tornado. Some of these ideas have been proven false. Don't believe these tornado myths:

The Open Window Myth

It was once thought that opening a home's windows before a tornado hit would protect the house. People knew that the air pressure inside the home was higher than the air pressure of the tornado. With the windows closed, they thought the tornado could make the house explode. Opening the windows was thought to protect the house by making the pressure equal.

Fact:

While a tornado does have low air pressure, the low pressure does not damage a house. A tornado's high winds cause the damage.

The Hills and Rivers Myth

Some people think rivers or hills protect towns from being hit by a tornado. They believe that a tornado cannot cross the water or rise above hills.

Fact:

In reality, hills and rivers offer no protection. The town of Emporia, Kansas, sits between two rivers. It was hit by tornadoes in 1974 and 1990. During the tornado outbreak on April 3, 1974, tornadoes crossed a ridge 3,000 feet (914 m) high.

The Bridge and Overpass Myth

Some people think that seeking shelter from a tornado under a bridge or an overpass provides good protection.

Fact:

It is very dangerous to seek shelter from a tornado under a bridge or an overpass. A person can be hit by debris that blows under the bridge. A person could also be carried away by the tornado's winds.

On May 3, 1999, some people hid under overpasses when a tornado crossed interstate highways in Oklahoma. Many of them were killed or injured after being blown out of their hiding places or hit by debris.

The Southwest Corner Myth

People once thought the southwest corner of the basement was the safest place to be in a tornado. This idea was based on the observation that many tornadoes move southwest to northeast. People thought that debris would then fall into the northeast corner.

Fact:

Going to the southwest corner is not good advice. Walls could collapse on you or flying debris could be blown in your direction. Debris can fall into any corner, not just the northeast one. It's better to be under something that offers protection away from outside walls and windows.

Safety in the Aftermath

A tornado often leaves behind piles of splintered wood and jagged pieces of metal. There can be sharp objects in the rubble. Be careful when moving through tornado debris. Wear tough shoes, long pants, and a long-sleeved shirt to prevent cuts. Don't walk near severely damaged buildings. They could still collapse.

Other safety tips help prevent electric shocks and fires after a tornado. Stay away from power lines that have fallen. If there is a smell of gas or a hissing sound inside a building, get out quickly. Call the fire department or gas company to let them know a gas line might have broken.

Nothing can stop a tornado from coming. However, being prepared for its arrival can help keep you safe.

destruction from a tornado that hit Moore, Oklahoma, on May 8, 2003

damage from a tornado that struck Mississippi in November 2002

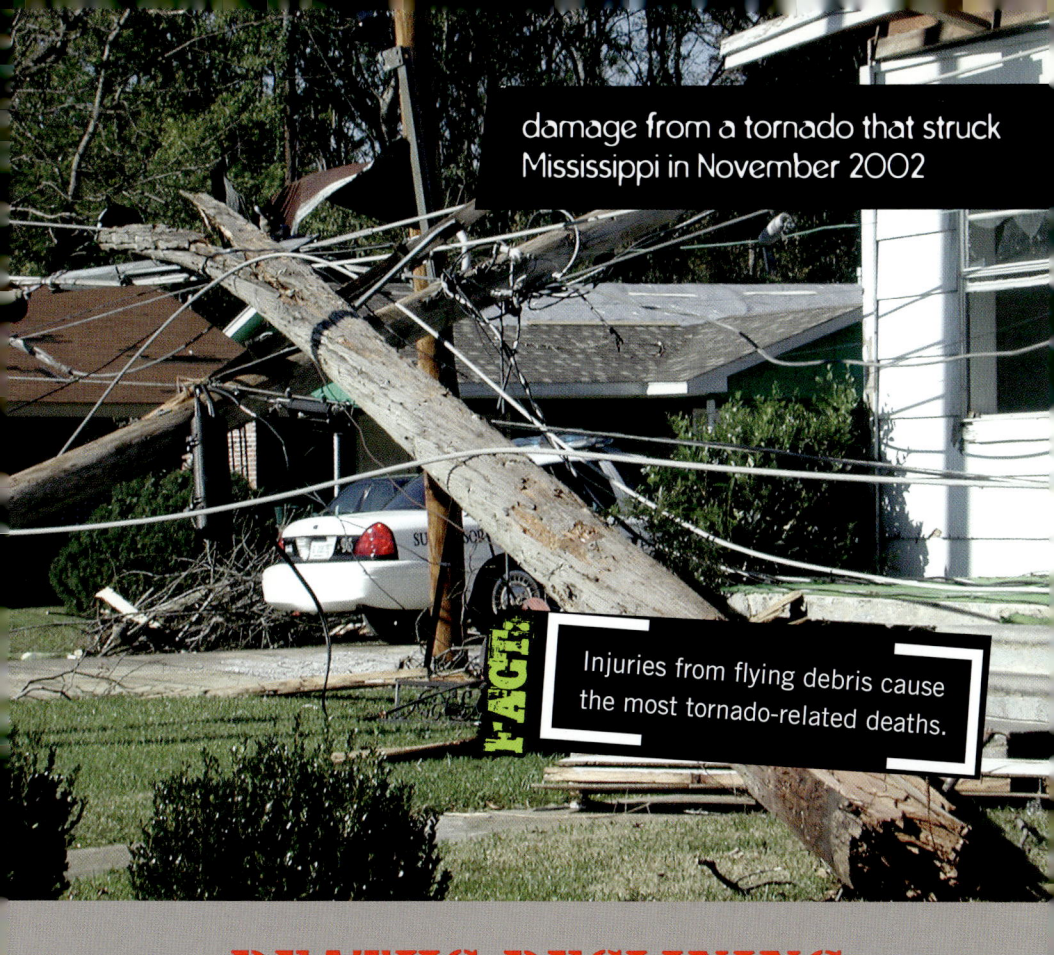

FACT: Injuries from flying debris cause the most tornado-related deaths.

DEATHS DECLINING

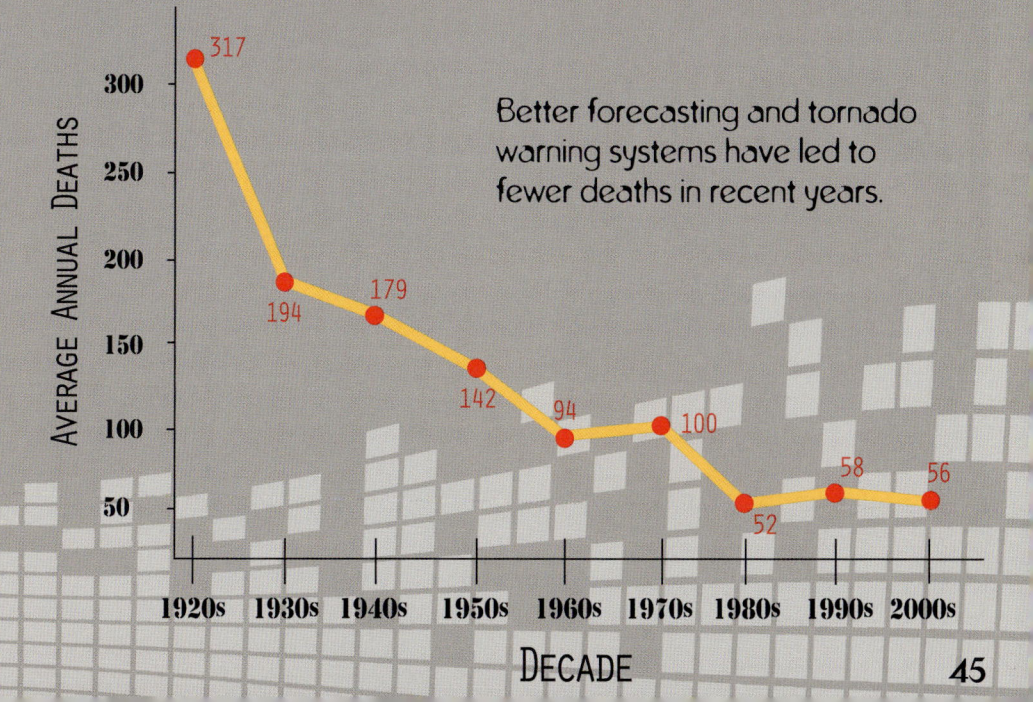

Better forecasting and tornado warning systems have led to fewer deaths in recent years.

Decade	Average Annual Deaths
1920s	317
1930s	194
1940s	179
1950s	142
1960s	94
1970s	100
1980s	52
1990s	58
2000s	56

GLOSSARY

air pressure (AYR PREH-shuhr)—the weight of air

condense (kuhn-DENS)—to change from a gas into a liquid

cumulonimbus (kyoo-myuh-loh-NIM-bus)—a tall cloud that produces a thunderstorm

debris (duh-BREE)—the remains of something that has been destroyed

downdraft (DOUN-draft)—a downward movement of air

funnel cloud (FUHN-uhl KLOUD)—a spinning column of air that hangs from a larger cloud but has not touched the ground

hail (HAYL)—balls of ice that fall during some thunderstorms

humidity (hyoo-MIH-duh-tee)—the measure of the moisture in the air

mesocyclone (mez-oh-SY-klohn)—a spinning column of air in a supercell thunderstorm

satellite (SAT-uh-lite)—a machine that circles the Earth; satellites send and receive messages from Earth

suction vortex (SUHK-shuhn VOR-tex)—a small but intense swirling column of air within a tornado

tornado warning (tor-NAY-doh WOR-ning)—a message issued by a local National Weather Service office when a tornado is seen by spotters or on radar

tornado watch (tor-NAY-doh WATCH)—a message issued by the National Weather Service when conditions are right for a tornado to occur in an area

updraft (UHP-draft)— an upward movement of air

vortex (VOR-tex)—a tube of spinning air

READ MORE

Gifford, Clive. *Chasing the World's Most Dangerous Storms.* Extreme Explorations! Mankato, Minn.: Capstone Press, 2010.

Martin, Michael. *How to Survive a Tornado.* Prepare to Survive. Mankato, Minn.: Capstone Press, 2009.

Silverstein, Alvin. *Tornadoes: The Science Behind Terrible Twisters.* The Science Behind Natural Disasters. Berkeley Heights, N.J.: Enslow Publishers, 2010.

Spilsbury, Louise, and Richard Spilsbury. *Hurricanes and Tornadoes in Action.* Natural Disasters in Action. New York: Rosen Central, 2009.

INTERNET SITES

FactHound offers a safe, fun way to find Internet sites related to this book. All of the sites on FactHound have been researched by our staff.

Here's all you do:

Visit *www.facthound.com*

Type in this code: 9781429654944

INDEX

air pressure, 21, 24, 42
anvil, 9
Argentina, 16

Bangladesh, 17

Canada, 14, 16
chickens, 30, 31
color, 11, 12
condensation, 6, 12

deaths, 4, 16, 17, 28, 32, 33, 36, 43, 45
Dixie Alley, 14
Dominator (storm-chasing vehicle), 24–25
downdrafts, 7, 8, 9, 10, 28

Enhanced Fujita (EF) Scale, 26, 27, 38, 39

forecasting tools, 20–21
    computer models, 20
    Doppler radar, 20
    satellites, 20
    turtles, 21
    weather balloons, 21
Fujita Scale, 27, 38
Fujita, Tetsuya "Ted," 27
funnel clouds, 10–11, 22

Great Britain, 16

hail, 6, 7, 20, 22, 23, 36
humidity, 21, 24

lightning, 6, 7
Loomis, Elias, 31

mesocyclones, 8, 10
mobile homes, 41
multiple vortex tornadoes, 12
myths, 42–43

National Weather Service (NWS), 18, 19, 21, 22, 26, 36

oddities, 30–31
outbreaks, 36–37, 38, 42

safety, 40–41, 42–43, 44–45
severe weather risk levels, 19
shapes, 13
South Africa, 17
storm chasers, 22, 23, 24–25
Storm Chasers (television show), 24
Storm Prediction Center, 18, 19
storm spotters, 22
suction vortices, 12, 29
supercells, 8–9

thunder, 7
thunderstorms, 6–7, 10, 14, 17, 18, 19, 21
Tornado Alley, 14–15
tornado formation, 6–7, 8–9, 10
tornado seasons, 5, 16
tornado shelters (buildings), 41
tornado stages, 10–11
tornado warnings, 19, 40, 41, 45
tornado watches, 19

updrafts, 6, 7, 8, 9

weather radios, 40